Chippendales
The Naked Truth

Troy Kline and Joe Bice

PACIFICA PRESS

Pacifica Press
P.O. Box 1780
Mercer Island, WA 98040

Library of Congress 98-068184

ISBN 0-9668096-0-2

Printed in the United States of America
1   3   5   7   9   10   8   6   4   2

Chippendales
The Naked Truth

1

In the summer of 1979, a tall, 34-year-old native of Bombay, India, Steve Bannerjee, discovered while living in Los Angeles that American women had fantasies about men and the mystique of well-developed male bodies. Though this revelation didn't rate up there with pasteurization and a cure for tuberculosis, it was a not-so-well-hidden secret. At singles bars, an American institution he appreciated, women gave men a top-to-bottom once-over, checking chests, muscles, behinds, and crotches.

Crotches! Oh my God!

Such female perusal would never have been tolerated in old Bombay or anywhere in the Middle East for damn sure. He wasn't positive about the rest of the world. But in America? Anything was allowed, perhaps not condoned, but allowed nonetheless.

Nice girls, ladies, and *good* women were supposed

to keep their eyes, like their skirts, down at all costs. The last thing the older generation ever wanted was sexually assertive women knowing, much less talking, about orgasms, their right to erotic pleasure, men's sexual potential or performances, or the fact that they found men's bodies provocative and stimulating to watch and feel.

They'd come a long way since bustles and hoop skirts!

And Steve Bannerjee was the disciple who pushed the envelope for the American women's liberation movement.

He had an original idea. The land of the free liked original ideas. What about a new twist on the old bump and grind, using males instead of females, attracting a "ladies-only" audience. What a concept! But would women come out of their shells to fork over real money when men peeled out of theirs?

Steve borrowed $1,000 from a fellow enthusiast and leased an empty, former strip nightclub building sweating its way into termite oblivion. It had been abandoned for two years in a low-rent business neighborhood of West Hollywood. He didn't have the money to renovate the sleazy interior like he wanted; a spit shine would have to do. A few buckets of dark blue paint and a repair of the runway did wonders for the old stripper watering hole.

He and his partner repaired the loose boards on the stage, added a wallpapered backdrop of a nighttime scene blinking with sparkling stars, and sent for the Orkin man. Steve purchased well-rehearsed tables and chairs from another defunct club for a song, giving him enough music to seat eighty people on a good night. White tablecloths and potted geraniums added their own notes to the scale. The bar leaning against the far wall, recovered with matching blue vinyl, completed the score.

An excellent sound system was the next hurdle. Fortunately, his new partner had good credit. Everything in Steve's great American dream depended on rock music to caress and stimulate the audience into frenzied participation. This essential ingredient was located and installed in record time.

What about a liquor license? That took big bucks. Steve and his partner didn't have big bucks.

So if you don't have a license, you come up with an angle to get one. Steve's angle was a club membership fee. Get a hundred women at 25 bucks a throw for admittance anytime into the club, and you have $2,500 before one can shake a well-tanned ass.

That is, if the women went for his concept!

They did in great numbers . . . more than 300 at first try.

Now all that was missing were the exotic dancers. Instead of the usual silicone beauties traditional in strip joints, Steve interviewed muscle men from local gyms, wannabe film actors working their way through weight-lifts and treadmill machines, stretching abdominal and leg muscles to the limit. If women liked to look at the boys, Steve would give them young Schwarzeneggers to ogle.

He chose his performers carefully, requiring applicants to strip to their Jockeys and pose, then do a bit of bump and grind, male-style. The auditions were hilarious. Most couldn't dance their way down a hopscotch silhouette without stepping on the line. Many had little or no rhythm except for pumping iron. When they tried to strip from fantasy costumes facilitated by Velcro closings, they looked like Al Bundy trying to act cool. Not to worry! Rehearsals would circumvent dance devils. The Los Angeles Ballet wouldn't have to worry about losing its *Swan Lake* audience.

Over all, Steve was after the "look," the sensual, come-hither countenance. His dancers must be no more than 25 years old, have good bodies, and be at least six feet tall. Women liked their idols young and muscular, but lofty in stature. Hair length could vary, though he favored long locks. After all, Beatlemania had legitimized Samson-like hair for men. His beauties must be clean-shaven and devoid of underarm, chest, and groin hair. He wanted no telltale pubic bush peeking obscenely from leg openings of thong bikinis.

Obtaining applicants for auditions was surprisingly easy. Word of Steve's endeavors spread like gym sweat around Hollywood's exercise emporiums. He interviewed more than 200 hunks, finally choosing ten dancers eager to work for tips and all the women they could lay. The opportunities seemed endless. Steve did nothing to discourage their wish list.

Next came his take-off of the Playboy bunny costume — collar, black bow tie, and black stretch pants so tight their religion was no longer in doubt. Starched white wrist cuffs accented muscular arms. Black leather boots could make a stomp-around statement better than loafers. The bunny tail was a piece of fluff he could do without.

Another ten Chips were hired as waiters and bartenders, all with the look, all working for tips — and whatever!

Even though Steve had sold more than 300 club memberships, having left flyers at beauty shops and women's clubs that would allow them, he never dreamed so many pearls would show up on opening night. Was a mistake his oyster? It wasn't. Nothing like public demand to create a sea storm tempest. He couldn't buy that kind of weather.

That first Friday night, Steve was nervous as a turkey facing a roasting pan. He had all the sea swell he could handle.

Two hundred or so screaming salt-of-the-earth women shuffled in line for the nine o'clock show, waving their membership cards like cowgirls at a groping contest. They could hardly wait to stuff bills in tiny waistbands en route to the promised land as guaranteed on the flyers.

How do 200 women fit into eighty seats? Not easily!

The ladies didn't take the lack of seats lying down. "Girlsterous" voices was the name of the game, so much so that Steve was forced to admit everyone, advising the last 120 or so, "Standing room only, please."

If the Hollywood fire marshal had been in attendance that night, Steve's original idea would have gone up in smoke.

With nothing more than handsome Chips in their bare-chested costumes hustling drinks and wiggling their way through the ladies, the enthusiastic audience began to scream, whistle, and clap. More than one waiter removed eager hands from taunting crotches.

Finally, the emcee announced, "Ladies, welcome to Chippendales. Fasten your seat belts. You are in for a bumpy night tonight!"

The show began with an anemic Las Vegas-style opener, a flashy dance routine including every man in the place — strippers, waiters, even the bartenders. Then the emcee entered the dance floor doing a reverse strip. Starting out in a thong bikini, he put it all on, then proceeded to work the crowd for the rest of the show, a series of vignettes loosely based on a "fantasy weekend": the accommodating Room Service Waiter, the Souvenir Man in a cage, the Macho Motorcyclist, the James Deanish Rebel who makes a cause out of oiling his body, and the Friendly Chauffeur, all performed with a tantalizing, hip-thrusting kind of delivery.

Steve had rehearsed the guys until they were ready

to drop more than their drawers. But his striplings mellowed. They sensed what Steve was after — something new to the nightclub scene. Eroticism with a touch of class. Could that be?

Above all, Steve wanted his Chips to seem gentle, macho, and available, there only to please the patrons. His goal was for women to simply succumb to the loving burlesque and have fun.

The Chips got all the attention of a Vegas showgirl and then some. Early on, a couple of over-enthusiasts climbed on stage and ripped the Velcroed bikini off one of the solo dancers. The thunder of audience approval rocked the rafters. Bodyguards would have to be hired during later shows to prevent such animalistic advances.

The unintentional total strip was a boon to business. Word got around quicker than the Watts Riot. The next seven nights, even with extra tables and chairs jammed around the dance floor, sweat had nowhere to fall except on the patrons.

By the time that first show ended, the women were bubbling, still shouting, no doubt wet in places they hadn't intended. That's when the *real* party began. Women, singly and by twos and threes moved onto the dance floor, gyrating bodies, letting the Chips fall where they might. By then, all the watered-down booze had hit bottom. Women were letting it all hang out, dancing with each other, energized and feeling a seemingly special high.

Steve was amazed, having fully expected the ladies to depart at the end of the show. Not so! More drinks — more money. Fantastic! Apparently the girls were adrenaline-high, being with so many other women and feeling the need to celebrate.

He then realized another truism that was to hold him in good stead throughout his Chippendale career. Where else could women go out and kick back like that? Maybe in a lesbian bar? He wasn't sure. But here, straight women were able to be publicly free in ways that seemed impossible, apparently without a concern of how they looked doing what they were doing, without giving a damn about men and about being hit on.

Where else, for a couple of hours, could women leave the real world of work, family, and cooking, and venture into a world of Samson-built, film-star-handsome men that they could get near — so near they could stuff money into a G-string straining with fantasy bounty? It was a fun place where women could feel special and appreciated as sexual individuals.

It wasn't until then that Steve suspected the club he had anointed "Chippendales" (named after the classic furniture known to represent sturdy and shapely frames) would become known far and wide, setting meek and lonely women in Los Angeles free — even some not so meek and lonely!

A year later, using the big bucks generated from "females-only-please" memberships (now 2,000 strong) coupled with exorbitant drink prices, Bannerjee's nightclub scene moved to larger quarters, four times the size of the original strip joint. The new club was deluxe — dark walls, flashing strobes, speakers blasting heavy-bassed hot disco, and utilitarian banquettes and benches lining the dance floor. Music videos and pin-ups of handsome, well-muscled young men in stock seductive poses adorned screens positioned around the room. A covey of young men flew through the eager crowds, serving drinks, hugging new arrivals, and smiling and joking with the customers ready and willing to molt.

Eventually, much of the rest of the female world would discover what all the Chip cheering was about.

Who would have guessed that this erotic male emporium of pulchritudinous sex symbols would grow to become a multimillion-dollar enterprise, spinning off an entire line of products: T-shirts, thong-style underwear, playing and greeting cards, sweatshirts, black bow ties, hats, calendars, videos, numerous clubs, and a Broadway-style fantasy show that would scandalize and titillate females all over the world?

The woman's night out, an enigma Dr. Kinsey would have applauded, had taken on new meaning.

"Chippendales" has subsequently become a household word and, despite legal and financial setbacks that have threatened to overthrow Bannerjee's estimable empire more than once, his exotic emporiums of male flesh are still touring legitimate stages — and some not so legitimate.

It's no wonder! Originally, Chippendales provided a revue where male dancers shook, shimmied, bumped, and stripped down to essentials — a thong brief for an almost exclusively female audience who waved dollar bills in the air for their favorites in exchange for sweaty hugs and kisses. In some cities, one could even order up a male stripper for house and office calls, to shake it down for private parties.

In November 1986, after nine years of scintillating nightclub performances, Bannerjee hired Steve Merritt to spruce up the shows with new choreography.

By 1986, the Chippendale image had suffered from a growing conservatism in response to AIDS. The disease changed the way men and women viewed erotica. The old way was very blunt, adopting a kind of "Me-Tarzan-you-Jane" approach to sexuality where the man was ultimately the aggressor and the one in control.

The new show, *Welcome to My Fantasy*, avoided type-casting the dancers as construction workers, policemen, lifeguards, etc. (staples of the old nightclub act) for men who projected an Eighties masculinity.

Welcome to My Fantasy opened at the Chippendale club in New York City in March of 1987. Andrew Lloyd Webber, move over! It was a resounding success, so much so that, for two weeks following the opening night, New York's off-duty finest had to be hired to keep the riot out front on simmer.

The show relied heavily on high-voltage, dance-oriented numbers featuring mainstream rock, pop, and heavy metal music. The movement blended martial arts with modern dance, gymnastics with jazz, ballet with break dancing.

The new acts were more sensual than sexual. Merritt had convinced Bannerjee that women had been placed in a position wherein they had to take responsibility for their relationships with men, even if the men didn't feel the same way.

The stage show became even better. A newly hired tour manager, Mark Pakin, masterfully elevated Chippendales from its Los Angeles success to what has become an international smash hit. Serving as manager for the initial U.S. and Canadian tour, Pakin later put Chippendales on the map in Europe, South Africa, Hong Kong, Australia, Guam, and the Philippines. The show's tremendous reception in England opened the door for what would be its stamp of credibility when the show opened at the Strand in London's West End.

Chippendales had become legitimate.

Today, the men of Chippendales are Broadway singers and dancers, theater arts graduates, recording artists, models, and, yes, former waiters, cab drivers, even hairdressers. They are extremely well-rounded men who love themselves and what they do. That love exudes into the audience.

The show has become a high-energy musical theater experience spiced with raunchy, seductive moments and almost all the nudity the female population can cream over.

It's truly a great night out for the girls.

Who would have thought an original idea and a thousand bucks would create such a female hurricane?

And I, Troy Kline, in January of 1993 — just a country boy from the little town of Wenatchee, Washington, six-feet-one-inch tall, with short, sun-streaked blond hair — slipped into this high-energy, explosive, raunchy, seductive musical theater experience.

2

I, Troy Kline, spent most of my formative years growing up in a Pentecostal Assembly of God religious family, attending church regularly with my brother and sister in Wenatchee, Washington.

My hometown, northeast of Seattle, fifty or so miles east of the Cascade Mountain Range, is a folksy farming community lying wishbone-like beyond the fork of the mighty Columbia River and its rapid-choked tributary, the Wenatchee. This eastern Washington spread embraces the Columbia before it snakes north, dividing apple orchards parading up its banks, then heads west to the even mightier Grand Coulee Dam near Spokane.

The Wenatchee Indian tribe first settled the community a hundred or so years previous, though they called themselves Pisquows. The word "Wenatchee" came from Shahapitian, loosely referring to the "water coming out" of the Tumwater Canyon near the town of Leavenworth to the west. The name was first used by white pioneers who, having stumbled upon the excellent fishing in the two rivers, decided to make camp and stay awhile. The climate, bitter cold in winter and stinging hot in summer, was also perfect for hunting black bear and deer. The pioneers eventually displaced the Wenatchee Indians to a government-sanctioned, bleak piece of reservation to the north.

My father's career was varied, from a carpenter to a fireman to a paramedic, depending on the year in question. My mother was a super-mom who worked all day to provide half the bacon. She came home, took care of us three kids, cleaned house, cooked dinner, and never complained about her lot in life. I grew up thinking that's why moms were invented.

Ever since I was a kid, I wanted to be a professional singer. I began my career at five by mimicking performers on television. I learned *Puppy Love* by Donny Osmond by listening to the record until there were no grooves left.

I was not bashful about my God-given talent. I'd perform for family and friends at the drop of a baseball hat, whether asked to or not.

My prowess as a stage-struck singer became a family joke. It was no joke! I was going to be a singer of renown. Nothing was going to stop me from conquering the big-time.

I loved the energy emanating from an audience, no

matter how small. Just performing for people was the kicker; the applause, recognition that I had talent. Was it enough to become a professional songbird? Any comment to the contrary ruffled my feathers.

At age 13, I realized that the Pentecostal congregation reacted to preaching in mysterious ways, speaking in what they called heavenly language, i.e., tongues. I doubted these strange sounds meant anything to them. The shouting and waving of appendages seemed to have little effect on the Lord, much less me. Divine healing via the minister's laying of hands on congregation members produced no surprises, and no miracles either. I was a logical thinker, too suspicious of Bible-thumping show business for my own good.

Even so, at age 16, while attending a Christian camp, I gave my life to God, having little knowledge of what such commitment entailed. All of the other guys my age were "succumbing to the will of the Lord," so it seemed the cool thing to do. I was told I could now start speaking in tongues at church. It hadn't made sense when I was younger, and it meant even less at sweet 16.

All this exhibitionist action during services was supposed to oust the demon from the unworthy. I wasn't so sure at that age that I didn't want to experience the wrath of that little ol' demon. I couldn't quite accept at face value some of the preachings of the dogma either. I couldn't understand why the Pentecostals were so against the Mormons and the Jehovah's Witnesses.

I suppose they resented any success the alternative religions had in the Bible-belting business.

My parents led me into the philosophy holding me captive in my tender years. I was not introduced to a color choice of opinions regarding religion and God. Perhaps the severe structure of this time of life instigated the first of my rebellions against home and church.

Though my speaking voice dropped to an expected level when I reached puberty, my singing voice remained high tenor. The contrast between pitches was startling, dramatic, and strong. I sang at local funerals, weddings, and parties. Everybody wanted me. Perhaps that was the beginning of an ego trip that in years to come bound itself to me like Trekkies to the Starship Enterprise.

My father supported my singing talent at every turn, as long as I traveled down the narrow road of gospel singing. His hope centered on my joining a Jimmy Swaggart type of evangelism, lending my voice to God. Little did I know that narrow road would become a costly freeway, a drive-by shooting of drugs and sexual excess as a stand-up singer in a male strip show traveling Europe.

I was a lead singer in the chorus at Wenatchee High School and attended jazz, classical, and barbershop singing classes. I hadn't the patience nor desire to learn to read music, a major hindrance throughout the start of my singing career. My ear was good enough to tune in notes and melodies and develop them into my own style.

While sweating out the grades at Wenatchee High School, I played baseball, ran track and cross country, and would have been on the swim team since we had a pool at home, but the school did not. Though I didn't excel at sports, I lettered. My ear was constantly tuned to the music ground. I was saving myself for Mr. Soul Public. I didn't know shit! But, who does in high school? What did History, English Literature, and Algebra have to do with Lionel Ritchie's success anyway?

What to do after high school graduation became the burning issue, flamed by desires for a singing career. "He succeeds who helps himself," right? Better learn a profession for the lean years.

My future wife, Linda, an attractive brunette with an easy-going personality who actually liked high school, was going to be a hair stylist, so what the hell, I would be also. I was attracted to her from the start by her winning smile and even temperament. We started dating while we were juniors. It wasn't surprising that we studied together for a year at The Academy of Hair Design in Wenatchee while she mastered her chosen profession.

In Wenatchee, if you dated a girl for more than a summer, you were expected to get married after high school graduation. We'd already stretched that rubber band by a year. So, at nineteen, in the spring of 1984, we succumbed to the pressure from church and family and married in a big church wedding — the works.

When was the world going to discover me? It wasn't likely in small-time Wenatchee singing in taverns with piano or karaoke accompaniment and praying some big recording studio executive would ride into town yelling, "Hi-yo Silver away!"

So now what, Lone Ranger? Better move to the big city.

Though Linda enjoyed Wenatchee living, she was game. She liked big cities and had even visited one once.

We moved to Bellevue, a suburb on the east side of Lake Washington, fifteen minutes from downtown Seattle. I abandoned most of my Pentecostal teachings. After all, when we leave the parental shelter, we become a hovercraft experimenting in new waters of morals and ethics, good, bad, or indifferent.

In Bellevue, I thought my entrance into the big time would best be facilitated by getting on the national TV program *Star Search*. I didn't have the expertise or the wherewithal to make a professional recording. Most importantly, I lacked Linda's support regarding my singing abilities. She knew I was good enough to make a career out of it, and therein lay the problem. She was afraid she'd lose me to that demanding public in the canyons of my mind. "You're a good hair stylist," she said. "Be content with curlers and hair spray. Leave the singing in church."

Even though I thanked God every day for the voice

he gave me, I think it kept me from any sort of success in business. In the recesses of my mind, I was standing in the wings waiting for a Lionel Ritchie angel.

I watched an anti-drug commercial on the local NBC affiliate, KING 5, one day, realizing it was really stupid. I could write a better song. So I worked at a tune, picking notes out in my head, scratched the lyrics down on an old cafe menu, working them over and over until the rhyming words jelled, then sang the resultant tune to a pianist buddy.

The result of all this frantic composing was a song called "Getting To Know," which I felt was perfect for use in the teenage anti-drug war. I called KING 5 a zillion times before I could get an appointment to play my solo recording. They liked it and agreed to use it.

A month later, they'd set up a filming at the Seattle Center with a bunch of hip teenagers. I actually lip-synced the song, having previously recorded it in a studio.

I loved recording. It was like creating perfection. Though there is nothing like the control and feeling you get in front of an audience, recording in a well-tuned studio is second-best. Just standing in front of a mike in a soundproof room with music blaring in your earphones with no one to disturb your concentration is a natural high.

We had about three weeks of rehearsals before filming "Getting To Know." For the next six months, it was aired on KING 5 many times. I was proud that 400,000 or so people saw it each time. I had volunteered my work for the Public Service Announcement, a good cause, my contribution to help keep kids off drugs.

It was ironic that I would get so involved with marijuana myself in Europe a few years later. I obviously ignored my own lyrics of wisdom.

I soon discovered that I wasn't ready for marriage. In retrospect, I don't think anyone 19 years old should make a lifetime commitment to someone. You don't know who you are at that tender age. I certainly didn't. Still, no one had divorced in my family as far back as the family Bible flyleaf could attest. I would stick it out.

Four years later, when Linda and I were 23 and I was contenting myself with a karaoke-singing shtick, we had a daughter, Rene, the light of my life. Marriage was all right for awhile; after all, it had produced a sweet, wonderful girl whom I cherished.

Two years later, our marriage was history. Six years of bickering and lousy sex was enough; there never had been bedtime chemistry between us. I don't think we were truly in love with one another, just infatuated. At that time of my life, I had thought Linda had the problem during intercourse. In looking back, I think it was me. I was interested only in *my* sexual needs, not hers or even ours.

Our difficulties were more mental than physical. Things got worse, and I ended up moving out. Six months later, we were divorced. We didn't own a lot. She kept the furniture and wedding gifts and custody of Rene. I was allowed visiting privileges every other weekend.

I was so down during this time that I decided to call Kurt, a buddy from high school. We'd had a few beers lately at Hunan Harbor, a karaoke bar in Seattle. He was now working for Pursuit of Excellence. I thought maybe joining the therapy-type full-week session of classes designed to instruct a person how to better themselves might give me a new outlook on life. I needed one for sure.

Two weeks later on a Monday morning in April of 1992, some 200 fellow attendees joined me, trudging into the large meeting room in a Bellevue office building. We were all reaching for the brass ring of self-improvement.

The group leader explained that his efforts would be to bring everyone out of their comfort zone that first morning. "We're going to hold up a mirror to ourselves to reveal all the ugly images," he said. "You may not like what you see. Of course, that's the whole idea. Only when you've seen the ugliness can you begin to turn it into beauty.

"Everyone must participate in all of our activities. If you are hesitant or don't intend to join in, quit now. Your entrance fee will be refunded."

The room was quiet. Everyone was here for body and soul.

One of the first tasks we were assigned was to go to a person to whom we felt attracted and tell them why we were attracted.

I was one of fifteen or so in line for a stunning five-foot-six-inch blonde girl in her twenties. When I reached the front of the line, I glanced at her nametag and stammered, "Joanie, you have the most beautiful blue eyes I've ever seen." What a dumb thing to say! Her return smile seemed sincere.

I went back to my chair and sat for fifteen minutes while people moved from one person to another. No one came over to me. It was frightening. Why wasn't anyone attracted to me? Perhaps it was because I acted unapproachable.

A great benefit came out of that week-long session — a wonderful new person in my life, Joanie. I asked for her phone number and called her the next week. Even though she had a boyfriend, we started dating. She soon broke up with the other guy because of me.

I thought we were both heading in the same direction for personal growth even though she, at 21, was five years younger than me. Apparently not. Our steady dating, including intimacy, didn't last. We broke up because she felt I wasn't ready for another commitment. After all, I was still suffering from guilt over my divorce from Linda. I was hardly good company. Because Joanie came from a divorced southern California family, it wasn't surprising she hadn't committed herself to a long relationship with anyone.

Fortunately, there was enough rapport lingering for us to stage a rally, seeing one another occasionally as good friends. I even asked her one day why we weren't married. Her answer was filled with promise: "In time. In time."

Over the next year or so before I left Seattle for Europe, we developed this sort of spiritual connection. In my mind, she became angel-like. She had an enormous softness about her. We'd see each other every couple of weeks for dinner or a movie. No sex, though.

I began to think of Joanie as my soulmate. She'd be the first person I'd call if ever I was in trouble, knowing she'd be there with support and friendship.

My ex-wife Linda meanwhile had fallen for a rough type of guy, Carry. She asked him to move in with her and Rene. I was surprised at Linda's choice. Not only was he not handsome, but he was a heavy drinker and female-basher. He was extremely jealous of my relationship with my daughter.

My concerns over his treatment of them came to a head one Christmas Eve after I picked up Rene to spend the evening with my sister and her family. On the way, Rene told me, "Carry wants me to call him Daddy." I lost it. I turned the car around and took Rene back home, then not so calmly asked Carry to step outside.

He did.

"Don't ever ask my daughter to call you Daddy again."

He looked me in the face and said, "Fuck you."

Push turned to shove. We got into a little fight, and he ran off. It was the worst Christmas of my life.

Right after that, I decided that I had to get away from Seattle or go out of my gourd.

But where would I go?

3

April of 1992 found me living in an apartment in Kirkland, a Seattle suburb snuggled along the curving east bank of Lake Washington. I was almost happy with my chosen profession, a daily grind hair styling at Hair Company on Front Street in Issaquah, with a following of loyal customers. I spent every other weekend with Rene. I was smoking a little pot, drinking too much, and picking up an occasional one-night stand. What else does a horny, lonely, 27-year-old bachelor do?

One Saturday about ten p.m., I decided to hit Cafe DaVinci's in Kirkland, my favorite late-night bar/"meat market" a block from Lake Washington.

One look out the window at the inclement weather and I started to bag the idea, have a couple of beers, and watch the boob tube. On second thought, I was lonesome, maybe feeling a little sorry for myself. I needed demonstrative people and a karaoke mike in my face.

Little did I know, a hand was guiding me that night toward a show business future.

The weather was worse than I thought. October nights can be frigid as hell in the Northwest. I was soon as cold as a winter raft enthusiast riding the rapids of the Wenatchee River. The icy wind stung my balls right through my jeans. My curling toes would have fit into Aladdin's shoes. The blowing rain was worse. I was wet before I reached the car.

My used Chevy Blazer started okay, oblivious to the elements. However, the windshield wipers had arthritis, arms dysfunctional to the point I had to occasionally poke my head out the window to see the street. Fortunately, the bar was only a few blocks from my apartment.

Later, after drying my hair beneath the men's room hand-dryer, I slid across the leopard vinyl of my favorite booth. The disco lights were splashing the pillars and black ceiling with a brilliant primary wash, an enticement for everyone to mingle, though the singles jamming the place needed no enticement for cruising one another. In the center of the room, the mirrors on the sphere revolving above danced in the directed light, giving drunken smiles a speckled measles look.

Since I was pretty popular at Cafe DaVinci's, it wasn't long before a few regulars shouted, "Your turn, Troy."

I smiled, feeling a bit warmer. At least someone appreciated my singing talent. Never one to turn down an invitation, I accepted the mike from the karaoke jockey, Tiger B., nodded, gave him my selection, then held it like a used all-night sucker with a few licks left. I leaned against the booth table, planted my feet on the bare concrete floor, and grinned for all the world like Michael Bolton in pain. I was on stage, albeit a smoky bar choked with naked noise and vulgar laughter. A tiny spotlight framed my upper torso, creating an on-stage illusion in my mind's eye.

Halfway through my version of Al Hibbler's familiar "Unchained Melody" of the Sixties, the cacophony stopped. Everyone was listening as I sang the bridge: "Lonely rivers flow to the sea, to the sea, I'll be coming home, wait for me." Such rapt attention always got to me, almost bringing a tear to my pale green eyes and an extra softness to my voice. I was really into it now, notes soaring: "Oh, my love, my darling, I hunger for your touch." It was as though the lyrics were written for me, my situation in life, right now, my needs!

Something magical happened. I don't know how to explain it. I felt every musical nuance, every syllable. I began the second chorus, unsure I could finish without breaking down. "The show must go on" grabbed me by the throat. I hit a high note, then trilled flute-like up and down the scale to the finish, "God speed your love to me."

One could have heard a beer gulp in the ensuing silence. Then came cheers, people standing at their tables, clapping and yelling my name.

The tingle erupted up my spine and spilled into my addled brain. I'd never felt an ovation like this one in my life. It was sincere, lingering like celebrity concert applause.

I didn't know it, but Dame Fortune had just tapped me on the shoulder.

After the clamor died and the drunken conversation slid into first gear, I collapsed into the booth, a bundle of sadness, laced with elation over what I'd just done. Why wasn't I on some big stage, wowing an audience instead of sitting here in a Kirkland bar drowning in my sorrows with glints of mirror reflections sprinkling my forehead?

"You have a wonderful voice," a woman shouted near my ear. "Where do you sing?"

She bent close so I could hear over the bar din. "New York? L.A.?"

"Just here and in my shower." My smirk must have displayed ironic justice.

"No! Can't be. You're too good for that."

I smiled. "Thanks for saying so. Join me for a beer?"

"Not right now."

After introducing herself, Betty edged into the seat opposite me. I was still a bit stung over the emotion that had enveloped me like a poncho during the song. However, emotion is short-lived when you have an interested, good-looking woman idling across from you. I was about to kick lonely in the butt.

"My boyfriend is Sam Davies. He used to be a Chippendale touring Europe."

I nodded, registering the word "boyfriend." Still, it sounded as though he was somewhere else. I said, "What's a Chippendale?"

"You know, the male strippers."

"Oh! Yeah, sure." So? Big deal. Why should I care?

An hour later, I cared.

After auditioning, so to speak, for the late-arriving Sam Davies, with a couple of more karaoke songs, he talked to me about trying out for the Chippendales in L.A. He had the works — contact number, who to talk to, how to act.

I discovered over late-night lasagna in the Cafe Italia in the lower level of Cafe DaVinci's that Betty had accompanied Sam on his European jaunt with the Chippendales, even starred in a skin-flick filmed in Amsterdam.

I looked up, my eyes not registering the arched blue ceiling painted with clouds, and sighed, then nodded. Why not at least try out? What did I have to lose?

Dame Fortune had knighted me with her sword.

Shortly thereafter, accompanied by a professional band, I made a tape of three songs in a Seattle recording studio and sent the cassette to Chippendales headquarters in Santa Monica, California. The odds of success with my first audition venture were something like winning the Washington Lottery. I later learned that thousands of men try to get auditions with the Chips each year, without success.

Unbelievably, only a week later, I received a letter requesting a videotape of myself, standing, walking, etc., no doubt needing a visual of my stage presence.

I borrowed a video camera and called my new friend, Sam Davies. He invited me to his apartment for a taping session. We filmed outside on a rare sunny day in November (if you know Seattle, you know how rare sunny weather is at that time of year). He knew just what they wanted. He'd been there, done that. I was surprised my Chippendale contact didn't want me to take my clothes off for the video, not even my shirt. His interest must lie in my singing talent. Good. Better than good.

I soon discovered the contact guy was really an asshole, bitchy and demanding on the phone. I suppose he had to be to eliminate the peel from the orange — to get the juicy part of applicants into focus.

Believe it or not, I was actually invited to Los Angeles for a final interview. Fantastic. The job involved singing my heart out in a Chippendale stage show touring Europe. Wow! Europe? I couldn't believe my luck.

This was my destiny — a forward move, that first bigger-than-life step in my show business career. But wait a minute, I hadn't been hired yet!

This kicker invitation got me moving faster than a

curve ball. I just couldn't handle what was going on at home anymore with the divorce and too many sad songs at Cafe DaVinci's clinging to me like old sweaters. Could I survive the coldness of that final interview? Would they take me out of my personal snowstorm and present me with a black bow tie and cuffs?

I was told that all the interviewees would have to strip to underwear during the auditions. I took care of that department, rushing over to the Bon in Bellevue to buy new Calvin Kleins. Boxer, brief, bikini, thong, in knit or woven cotton — what kind? I settled on Calvin's finest cotton-knit bikini, tight-fitting with no front seams. I even tried them on in the dressing room. The saleslady must have thought I was some sort of pervert. Nobody ever tries on underwear!

What about the size of a guy's dick? Was size one of the requirements to be a Chip? One had to strip after all. All the way? Naturally, I'd never seen a Chippendale show. All I knew was that women stuck money in some guy's underwear who was swinging his torso to a disco beat in a smoky nightclub. Although I had nothing to be ashamed of in the dick department, displaying it would have been something like Robert Schuller showing a porno film at the Crystal Palace.

What about skin tone? My God! I was as white as Mt. Rainier snow. A tanning salon was the answer. There was one just across the street from my beauty salon in Issaquah. Better do it naked. They might ask me to pull off my new Calvin Kleins.

Unfortunately, I was hungover that day from celebrating my good fortune the previous night at Cafe DaVinci's. Once in the Count Dracula coffin, I fell asleep. Fortunately, the attendant watched out for hungover clients as if he had fangs and was hungry for blood. He awoke me in time to flip over. A little stinging on the rear and I was ready for a strip interview, or so I thought until I looked at my nude self in my apartment's full-length mirror. Oh God! I was sizzling — overcooked. Red as a Waikiki Beach tourist.

Maybe the interview committee wouldn't notice.

I was ready for the big time.

Almost ready!

I hadn't told my parents what I was about to do. That wouldn't be easy.

Two days before I left for L.A., I drove over a snowy Stevens Pass of the Cascade Mountain Range to Wenatchee.

"What happened to your face?" was Mom's first question. She'd noticed my winter blush.

I thought quickly, "Went skiing last weekend. Too much sun."

So much for no one noticing!

After telling my parents what I intended, they just looked at me curiously.

Mom finally said, "Do you have to wear a furry costume?" They thought I was referring to the smart-aleck cartoon chipmunks, Chip and Dale, that I was going to be a singing version at Disneyland or something. It took a while to explain the difference. I wasn't going to be a singing chipmunk; I was going to be a singing Chippendale in a stage show.

They obviously thought I was walking in sinful directions and told me so in Pentecostal-eze. I knew I'd offended my father with my cavalier attitude toward a future of sin when a single tear rolled down his cheek. I'd hurt him. That troubled me, but not enough to give up my audition plans. I probably should have left it at Chip and Dale. Cartoon characters are easier to stomach, and the idea was a whole lot funnier. But I would be in Europe for at least a year if I got the job. They had to know where I was going to be, didn't they?

What they didn't know and would never understand was how important this opportunity was for me.

They were positive I was rushing headlong down the path to Sodom and Gomorrah, armed with a slingshot too small to smite Goliath.

But I was 28 years old. At 28, you gotta follow your own destiny, right? I decided this was mine. Not even Billy Graham himself was going to stop me.

The thought of not seeing Rene for awhile made me wince.

When I made my fortune, I'd have plenty of time to make it up to her.

On January 5, a smoggy day in Los Angeles, Carolyn Somebody, an unattractive employee of Chippendales with too many teeth, picked me up at LAX. She chewed gum like it was a requirement for the position.

Upon settling into the van, she said, "Wow! You certainly qualify in the Chip department. And I've seen a few Chips."

"You think so?"

"Know so. Narrow nose; sensuous green eyes with heavy eyebrows; high cheekbones; full, kissable lips."

She sounded as if she was describing a Chippendale calender man. Yes, I'd picked up one of their calendars in Seattle to see what the competition looked like.

Carolyn kept on with the encouragement. "You'll melt the females out there. Take my word for it. You've got the look."

I laughed. "Hope management thinks so, too. I'm mostly a singer though, not a stripper."

"And a voice, too. Dynamite! You're in, fella." She continued to chirp between smacks of her gum.

"From your mouth to management's ears."

An hour later, she delivered me to the Hollywood Arms in North Hollywood, a somewhat seedy but classic hotel swathed in palm trees. I was to meet all the other Chip hopefuls around the pool, flexing their muscles, improving their tans the natural way in anticipation of a successful audition.

I later found out that we were the finalists of more than 5,000 guys auditioning for only six Chippendale positions.

At this time of my life, I was a very insecure, not-so-young, punk hair stylist from Wenatchee who had been through an unhappy marriage and an emotional divorce. What was I doing around all these muscular body builders? I didn't even know how to dance. I was scared, worried that I wouldn't get the job and, if I did, that it wouldn't work out.

What would happen when they discovered I had lied about that little item called "being able to dance" during my last phone conversation from Seattle? I couldn't even do a two-step without bumping into someone, much less survive a line dance without bruised boots.

Later I discovered, much to my relief, that the committee auditioning us, which included Steve Bannerjee, Mark Pakin, and Steve Merritt, was more concerned about how I looked, with or without clothes on. Self-assurance when performing, as well as a good sense of rhythm and timing, was important. Other considerations included how my body tones melded and if I was sensual when I moved. At my first audition, I stood before them half-naked, about as sensual as a lobster on a seafood plate, and just as red!

Because I'd lied about my dancing abilities to get to the final interview, it was soon apparent to Steve Merritt, the choreographer, that I couldn't even spell the word "dancer." The others would be shown the moves once or twice and had them down pat. Not me! "Pat" was an illegal wetback sitting in the boat still offshore. I sweated like an immigrant over each step, thinking my green card would be history any minute.

The committee members looked like they were worried about me. It didn't look as though I had much of a chance even as a Chiplet. I chewed on that idea as three guys hit the showers. I was feeling wet already. The sweat poured down my cheeks. Was I next on the agenda to be told to clear out my locker?

As soon as they asked me to sing, I perked up. I punched in a Boyz II Men song, "End of the Road," on my tape player and started warbling. Everyone stopped what they were doing and listened. My confidence soared. The applause following told me I still had a chance at a stage career, however naked the truth might become.

Steve Bannerjee spoke in a heavily accented voice, "He has a beautiful voice. Very sexy. I like it. I think Troy will do."

What did he just say? Troy will do? Did he really just say that? Mother of God! I wanted to shout, but somehow contained my enthusiasm. Nobody else was shouting. Was this official?

"Draw up a contract for him," Steve said casually to Mark.

It was official! I was a Chippendale.

The next day, I was signed to a one-year contract with Chippendales, retroactive to January 1, 1993.

However, I was a barnacle attached to the bottom

of the pay scale, like the other five rookies. With all travel expenses included, I would kick down $750 a week base salary plus tips. I was told by some of the regulars that I could make extra money taking photos of the leads standing next to females each night after the show.

Some of the top Chips were reported to make more than $100,000 a year. I was told even this salary was a pittance compared to the $1,200 a night in tips soloists in the nightclub acts of Chippendales sometimes pulled in.

During my stay in Hollywood, Steve Bannerjee insisted I lift weights every day in the exercise facilities of our hotel. My muscle tone was out of tune with the rest of my symphony.

After being chosen for the tour, I got cocky around the other guys. I always did have a smart mouth. It was forever getting me into trouble. Ego was dueling with my insecurity. I'd say things like, "I'm the best singer these guys ever had," Chip on the shoulder bullshit like that. Not surprisingly, it pissed the other guys off.

Something must have been said to management, because Steve Bannerjee called me into his Santa Monica office one day and said, "Hey, Troy. If you want to be a part of the tour, better learn to keep your mouth shut and stay cool," adding a few other choice words for effect.

I got the effect. I stayed cool throughout the rest of my stay in Hollywood.

Several rooms of a dance studio a few blocks from the hotel were reserved for Chippendales for the month of January 1993. Lunch, low in calories, was catered in so we could rehearse nonstop, eight a.m. to five p.m. every day, six days a week. We rehearsed and rehearsed and rehearsed some more. "Five-six-seven-eight. Eyes right, left foot."

Most nights following our strenuous workouts, we'd haunt the L.A. clubs. Roxbury's was one of our favorites. We went to all the hot nightclubs, the ones who would only let in people who were somebody. We never had any trouble getting in. A bunch of six-foot Chippendale muscle men strutting their stuff down the sidewalk wearing tank tops and skin-tight jeans was enough ticket to get us into any club we chose. We even scoped out the Hollywood Tropicana Club, a female strip joint famous for its mud-wrestling show. I met one of the wrestlers. It turned out she was staying in our hotel while doing a layout for *Hustler* magazine. I slid my way into her hotel room the next night. Though a quiet type, she showed me some of her nude studies. Very studious — explicit sex shots right out of *Deep Throat*. That night, I found out how deep still waters ran. She favored giving head. Okay by me!

Two days before we left Los Angeles for Copenhagen, two fifty-gallon Hefty Bags showed up at the studio where we rehearsed.

"What's that, Ernie?" I asked.

My new friend, one of the leads, volunteered, "A little gift from management."

The bags contained hundreds of packages of condoms. I laughed as we all loaded up. It was going to be a prophylactic journey as we rode our way into Scandinavia's more scenic curves.

4

On February 1, 1993, I was on a Boeing 747 heading for Copenhagen via New York's Kennedy and London's Heathrow airports. The first day of the rest of my life was beginning.

"Ecstatic" became a new word in my vocabulary, a feeling that would be short-lived.

As the plane flew into Denmark that sunny morning, my body tingled with anticipation. I was a bit worried about not being as muscular as the Chippendale show leads; however, I was a Chip now and apparently not too hard to look at. After all, the lead singer didn't have to be a calendar model flexing ab muscles and posing for every media opportunity. At 28, what better job could a horny man ask for than gyrating and singing his way through *Chippendales: The Scandinavian Tour* musical revue each evening?

Though I was beat from lack of sleep on the long

trip from Los Angeles, I peered out the airplane window, eyes wide. I was like a kid savoring his first Halloween trick-or-treat night. I'd never been outside the United States, other than to Canada.

The spire of Christiansborg, the seat of the Danish Parliament, glistened. Snow blanketed rooftops in puritanical white as far as I could see, accenting picturesque blue, ice-covered canals shimmering like crystal in the sunlight. No ugly skyscrapers punctuated the heavens, just graceful spires and domes jutting from block-long buildings as if they'd been daubed on at the last minute a couple of hundred years ago by frustrated architects with overzealous clients.

From a brochure I had picked up at a travel agency in L.A., I knew Copenhagen to be the largest city in Scandinavia. It prided itself on clean streets, lack of air pollution, and no traffic jams. I promised myself I'd find the time to see if this old city with its abundance of historical and cultural sights lived up to its publicity.

That morning, as the cast disembarked the bus at the Faulkner Hotel and Convention Center in the heart of Copenhagen, a cheer went up. I quickly discovered the true meaning of female groupies. Fifty or so twittering Danish teenagers and ladies in their twenties shifted anxiously on the sidewalk and in the hotel lobby, panting away for our much-ballyhooed arrival.

I was awed by the uninhibited adoration, shouts of glee, and waving limbs. Obviously, the women had been revved up by the Chippendale public relations department prior to our invasion of Denmark. Security men actually had to clear a path for us into the hotel.

Of the seventeen Chips in our company, three of the dancers were gay. At the Faulkner lobby desk, Brent, one of the gay dancers with clear blue eyes and slightly protruding ears, was assigned as my roommate throughout the tour. Though I had joined Chippendales only a month earlier and had fewer rights than a prop man, I was immediately pissed. Everyone else had been previously paired up, including the other two gays.

Hell! I wasn't about to accept a homo for a roomy.

Everything I'd been taught as an Assembly of God congregation member back in Wenatchee indicated homosexuals were the work of the devil, the closest thing to the Antichrist. All of them were unnatural humans, anything but normal, and must be steered clear of at all costs due to their infectious disease. The words had been drummed into my youthful head as fact, part of the ABCs of church doctrine.

I complained bitterly to Mark Pakin, the tour manager, flat out refusing to share the same hotel room with Brent. Mark's comment was, "If you want to pay for a private room yourself, go ahead. Otherwise, deal with it."

The rooms at the Faulkner Hotel were $200 a night. I'd have to deal with it, but I liked it about as much as all the shots we had to take prior to leaving the United States.

My attitude was problem enough to get Brent and me off on the left foot right off. Stormy seas ahead was an unfulfilled promise.

Following dinner that first evening, after too much wine and beer in the Faulkner bar, I bitched to Darrell, one of the Chippendales I'd befriended in L.A., about my tour sleeping arrangements. Darrell was one of the seasoned leads, dark hair styled like a hip teenager, dimpled chin, and narrow nose poking heavenward most of the time.

Darrell said, "No fuckin' big deal. He'll leave you alone. You leave him alone. We're all family here."

The words were hard to accept. I had never been around homos before. I was afraid Brent would jump-start his engine, then try my piston given the first opportunity. And he would be just an arm's reach from my bed every night. I'd have to sleep with one eye open and one hand on my crotch. My ideas were church-archaic to say the least. Naiveté was a word I would have to kick into the trashcan.

I would later discover the truth of Darrell's words. The company would become a closely knit group — all colors, creeds, religions, and sexual preferences accepted without rancor.

A few minutes after Darrell's sage advice about fellow Chips, I eyed an attractive blonde across the bar room returning the honors. Did lust just whistle? It was want at first sight.

"Pardon me, man. I think opportunity just rapped on my door." I nodded at the blonde.

Darrell smiled. "Careful, neophyte. Don't let that door slam on your dick." He laughed, slapped me on the back, and sent me on my way with a couple of condoms snuggling in my pocket.

When I reached her whistle stop, I quickly discovered Ellen was not a reserved study, nor a shy one. One step forward, and she was a high-speed locomotive all steamed up and heading down the track. It took me less than a second to figure Ellen meant business when she groped my crotch from a foot away. I was a fast learner!

She was easily as drunk as I. She pulled my hand to her breast and gave me a French kiss that made my dick as steely as the Eiffel Tower.

She asked, "Where's your room?"

"Upstairs."

"Let's go."

I didn't need a conductor to tell me where this train was heading.

Without bothering to ask Brent, my gay roommate, if I could use our tenth-floor room for my first European tryst, I just barged in and pulled Ellen onto one of the queen-sized beds into a lustful embrace. She was a Danish dish, a bowl overflowing to the rim who had perfected French kissing into an art form even De Gaulle would have appreciated. Though I was not an exhibitionist yet, I was too busy to care that Brent was watching from a few feet away. Lust had taken me by the dong and dug in.

I decided right away Brent was pissed when he threw a pillow at me and yelled, "Get that slut outta this room."

I told you I was a fast learner!

My erection wouldn't be denied. I yelled back, "Don't have any other place to go."

"Well, you sure as hell can't stay here. This is my room, too." He gave me a dirty-dare look and threw another pillow.

With an impatient glare, I pulled Ellen, looking like a porno movie siren, sweater around her neck, bra crinkling around her waist like two deflated balloons, off the bed, stiff-marched her into the bathroom, and slammed the door.

Shit, that bathtub was cold! We both complained loudly, though such protestations quickly metamorphosed into moans of passion. The position that I didn't learn in a mission was about all we could pray for in this porcelain maim meadow.

What was Brent doing about all this moaning? Sitting on the edge of the bed on the other side of the door dialing Mark Pakin, our tour manager, in order to bitch his head off about my "tit-a-tit."

Before Ellen and I had reached the impossible dream, Mark Pakin banged on the bathroom door. "Get the girl out of there, Troy. This is Brent's room, too, and he doesn't like what's going on."

Shit! Just like the fag. I was just finding the right rhythm, even humming a little. That was all she wrote. My hard-on wilted like a candle left out in the sun too long.

If it had been later in the tour, I would have told both Mark and Brent to "fuck off" and completed my first tour of duty.

But I was a freshman Chip on this first night in Copenhagen and expected to take my hazing like one. With a horny sigh, I told Ellen she'd have to hit the showers. No! We were already in there.

After showing Ellen the hall door, giving her a rain check in the form of my unfilled condom (she asked for it), I turned back into the room to receive my first lecture from Mark about the privacy rights of room-mates.

Later, after he left, I said a few choice words to Brent and added a half-assed apology. After calming down, Brent and I agreed that, in the future, neither of us would bring dates to the room (mine female, his male) unless we arranged it ahead of time.

My first night on the continent, I fell asleep with blue balls harder than a week-old Danish.

My feelings and attitudes were to change dramatically on the open tour road to Chipdom.

Hell, did they ever!

5

The morning following my arrival in Copenhagen and my tryst turnabout in the Faulkner Hotel bathtub with the Danish babe, I joined several other Chips heading down the tenth-floor hall toward the elevator. All of us were to meet in the lobby restaurant for breakfast. The minute the elevator doors opened on the ground floor, dozens of squealing girls came running across the lobby for autographs. This star thing was better than the cream center of an Oreo.

The other Chips, having been through this cookie cutter many times over, merely brushed off the fans with a wave, bared camera-ready teeth, and charged on into the restaurant. Not me. I spent time talking to the girls, getting to know them. They were fans after all. And I was a Chip off the new block.

To my delight, the scene was repeated every morning during our Copenhagen stay.

Each Chippendale tour group of the three traveling Europe the rest of the winter of 1993 had seventeen performers in the show, including dancers, singers, stripper leads, and master of ceremonies. The rest of the total thirty members in each company was made up of lighting men, wardrobe, stagehands, dance and vocal trainers, and security men hired in Europe.

I was the lead singer of four in my company, so I did the solos. The other singers danced as well. With my limited two-step, I danced in the opening and closing numbers only, a blessing for all concerned.

The first full day in Copenhagen was spent rehearsing on the Faulkner Theater stage for opening night.

"Five-six-seven-eight . . . left, right, up, down. Five-six-seven-eight . . . turn, turn, right, left."

The choreographer was relentless. "Take it on the downbeat, you weenies. Make it strong! Five-six-seven-eight . . . left, right, feet cross. Shoulders back. Push, push, step, step."

I felt those instructions down to my toes; unfortunately, my feet didn't.

That opening night, my hangover from all the booze the previous night made me as nervous as the Wicked Witch of the West waiting for Dorothy to drown her with a bucket of water. I think the water would have melted me, too, as I paced in the dressing room. Butterflies were having their way with my queasy stomach.

Larry, nymphomaniac of the company, dumb blond type, sat calmly in front of the mirror shaving his entire body, everywhere, pits, crotch, and chest. He always walked around naked, especially proud of his buns as if the paparazzi might invade this private sanctuary any minute and start snapping away. He obviously didn't want to chance missing that Kodak Moment of posterior posterity.

"Do I need more oil on my ass, Troy?"

I glanced at Larry. "You planning for an invasion back there?" The other guys laughed.

"No, stupid. It's for the stagelights. Got to moon the ladies!"

I sang, "Shine on, shine on harvest moon. . . ."

I moved my pacing to the stage wings. I didn't need to peek out the curtain to tell the house was jammed to capacity. The screaming rivaled that of teenagers at a Rolling Stones concert.

Opening night jitters, following my previous evening's debacle in the hotel bathtub, traumatized me. "Break a leg" took on new meaning.

We were about as ready to open in Copenhagen as a pre-Broadway show staged in Walla Walla. Though we could use more days of rehearsals, countdown zero was approaching with alacrity, allowing for no stand-down time in the wings.

To make matters worse, I didn't know all the lyrics to my songs. I wasn't even given the damn things until we were halfway across the Atlantic. Ever try to rehearse lyrics while strapped in an airplane seat at 30,000 feet between two six-foot-two guys?

The show started with Hollywood-like spotlights scrambling back and forth across the "CHIPPEN-DALES" letters on the front curtain. The music tempo picked up, followed by pyro explosions on each side of the stage. The ladies started cheering.

Mark Pakin made his voice debut on the mike from backstage. Tradition gave him the words: "Ladies, fasten your seat belts. It's going to be a bumpy night tonight."

The music exploded.

"Get out of your chairs, get up on your feet," the taped music blared. "Put your hands together, gonna feel the beat. . . ."

The girls at the front stood and started clapping to the music, then jutting their arms vertically into the air between claps.

"We're feeling all right . . . we're gonna rock the walls tonight."

The entire audience followed the actions of those in the front rows until the curtain rose.

Five dancers in jeans and half-jerseys with "Chippendales" stenciled on them bounced across the stage executing movements Gregory Hines would have been proud of.

A minute later, they exited stage left where I stood.

Audience clamor announced three Chips slinking side-step onto stage right, totally nude, dragging white towels like security blankets, oiled buns flashing in the bright lights — especially Larry's!

The naked truth was exciting enough to get a rise out of the crowd. The girls, still on their feet clapping to the deafening beat, started whistling. I thought only men put their lips together like that.

This was going to be a night Copenhagen would remember.

The nude Chips wrapped the towels around flexing butts, private parts casually draped while they clutched terry together with a free hand. They continued their practiced slink to center stage, then stood forward, one at a time, eyes toward the audience, smiles steaming with sex appeal. In sync, they rubbed their postpubescent protrusions through the towels seductively, turned to the side, slid an end corner of a towel down to cover their genitals, and started off stage left.

Had their part in the opening number ended at that precise moment, it would have been enough for the ladies out front.

However, Larry, the middle Chip, suddenly stopped. He'd stepped on the end of his towel, accidentally jerking it from his clutching fingers. Oh my God! He was naked facing 3,500 horny ladies. What to do?

Larry simply stopped, stepped off his towel, bent forward, and retrieved the terry cloth.

Not a good idea! Jerry, carefully choreographed to be directly behind Larry, bumped into Larry, knocking him to the floor in a heap. Miraculously, Jerry maintained his towel and kept right on prancing while Larry pulled himself upright, towel in place, face a darker shade of red than before as he followed the others off stage.

Despite the amps, our prerecorded voices were almost drowned out by the thunderous shrieking and laughter out front as the nude Chips made their way into the wings.

Five dancers entered, a chorus line of males in their prime, flailing arms and hands in time to the continued heavy-metal rock beat.

As the dancers faded off stage right this time, four lead Chips in jeans and sports jackets of different hues — lime green, shocking pink, royal blue, and lavender — stood spread-eagled center stage and stripped off their coats to the beat, bare, oiled chests glistening. The cheers increased in volume.

Finally it was my time, along with the other five Chips not yet introduced to the audience. We entered stage left, wearing jeans and half-jerseys, followed by another group of five from stage right, wearing leather biker gear. Seventeen strong, we danced the beat to the finish of the number, each turned on by the super-enthusiasm of the audience.

Nobody else tripped. Nobody was hit with a flailing appendage. A few motions were out of sync, but not so much so that the audience complained.

The opening number ended with whistles and cheers enough to encourage us all to drop our drawers. We didn't, however. Later, Mary. Later.

Blackout.

The lights glared, revealing a backdrop of a human torso shot. A pair of jeans from the waist down stretched across the entire stage. In the center, a twenty-foot zipper unzipped a few feet at the top, awaited the grasping hands of Superwoman.

This was my big moment. I entered stage right holding my hand-mike so tight that my knuckles went white. I couldn't see a thing beyond the stage, but heard plenty. My heartbeat pounded in my ears, almost eclipsing the sound of the accompaniment to "Drift Away."

"Day after day I'm more confused. But I look for the light in the pouring rain." Hey! I sounded pretty damned good. This wasn't so hard. The confidence oozed into my voice as I continued singing, gesturing with my free hand. The T-shirt tucked into my jeans was getting damp from perspiration. Fortunately, the wetness was covered by an open-front plaid flannel shirt with the long sleeves rolled above the elbows.

After I sang a few bars, Ernie entered stage left singing, "You know it's a game that I hate to lose. Feeling no pain, ain't it a shame." Everything went smoothly as we harmonized on the chorus: "Give me the beat, boy, to free my soul. I want to get lost in your rock 'n' roll and drift away."

We headed into the audience from separate stairs, blue spotlights beaming us down. We each chose a good-looking woman, sat in her lap, then planted a sweaty kiss on her. Then, like good Samaritans, we arm-wrestled two girls up on stage, still singing to them.

They were more than willing to follow.

At the end of the number, for the sake of show business, we took the girls backstage as though we were going to have sex. Then a security guard escorted the girls back into the audience. In later performances, if I wanted more than that sweaty kiss from mine, I'd tell the security guard to inform the recipient to meet me after the show.

No more mishaps occurred during the next two numbers other than a missed cue or two. But midway in the first act, the stagehands committed a doozy.

A recorded female voice announced, "Welcome to Hotel Chippendale, where they satisfy all your needs."

Six dancers in bellboy uniforms, one of them being Brent, my roommate with piercing pale blue eyes and Clark Gable ears, rushed determinedly on stage. Brent did everything with determination, applying makeup, shaving his mostly hairless body, especially performing. He was a stickler for perfection. He joined the others singing in front of the jean curtain: "Welcome, welcome, we're glad that you're here. Let us take care of you, dear. Listen, listen, we're at your command, just leave it all in our hands."

Unfortunately, they hadn't rehearsed with the Fourth-of-July-type pyro, bombs, explosions, sparks, and flashes added to the Hotel Chippendale scene.

Neither had the stagehands. A resounding clump backstage made the dancers center stage almost jump out of their uniforms.

Unknown to anyone, the prop men had lowered the Hotel Chippendale backdrop (a facade of a hotel) too fast behind the front jean-curtain. The jeans scrim rose to revolving doors in place center stage, but no hotel entrance scene. Our star lead, Russell, entered mid-stage through the back curtain in his doorman uniform smiling his worth, then fell over the unexpected prop into the revolving doors. He clung to the life-saving door frames, then slid to the floor, sprawling onto his brass buttons, cursing.

The backdrop was quickly raised to gales of female laughter. Much to Russell's credit, he refrained from giving the stagehands the bird and flew right into his routine, lip-syncing the words to the number. It was a good thing I was offstage singing. How I maintained on mike without breaking up is the wonder of the ages.

The chorus added, "So come in, come in, service with a smile. We'll go that extra mile. Welcome, welcome. . . ."

That extra mile was a long one.

During intermission in the dressing room, the guys joked and laughed at the blunders. Mark Pakin did not. After yelling at the stagehands, he came looking for us. The laughter stopped.

"Do you guys think this is fun and games? Believe me, it isn't. This is a very expensive show, and those are paying customers out there. We owe them more than you're giving them!"

He lowered his voice. "Try to be more careful. You can do this show blindfolded. You did it in rehearsals. Just do it again, that's all, and everybody will be happy."

His tone was no longer belligerent, just logical. He added a few compliments, even patted me on the shoulder. "Good opening number, Troy." He was now a mellow coach who meant business. He knew not to kick ass on opening night so much that resultant spite dancing would enter the equation.

Later, in the second act, I had already determined I couldn't get to my dressing room and back for my cowboy costume change in time, so I stripped from my *Grease* number leather pants with the help of a wardrobe lady in the wings. Oops! My Calvins came off with the tight leather. No time to worry about it. The wardrobe lady had seen everything many times over. I pulled on jeans and a western shirt.

With an extra pair of fumbling hands tying my chaps on, I rushed on stage, ready to sing "Born to Boogie."

Unfortunately, the musical accompaniment was that for the Tom Cruise number. "Old Time Rock and Roll" was blasting my ears, the number resurrected for Tom Cruise's dance in his film *Risky Business*. Everyone imitated Tom wearing white Jockey underwear, flicking the tails of their open pink dress shirts, and stomping their white cotton crew socks across the stage. They all glanced at me through their Ray-Bans as though I were Pee Wee Herman in drag.

Mother of God! Wrong scene!

I bravely switched horses, singing "Old Time Rock and Roll" while trying with one hand to artfully pull off my vest and shirt, alternating palms gripping the mike as though it might get away.

A few of the Chips on stage laughed, but carried on without missing a step of a crew-socked foot.

Finally, I got my upper clothing off and was naked to the waist. The crowd assumed I would strip to my Jockeys like the others on stage. Better do just that. I managed to untie my chaps to the beat and stepped out of them. I even unbuckled my cowboy belt. Whups! No underwear! Staying in role, I just shook my head at the audience, wagged a "no-no" finger, and kept on singing.

Overall, that first two-and-a-half-hour show was dynamite. Proof: an explosion of a standing ovation at the end, all that a bunch of sober Chippendales could hope for.

6

We continued to practice on stage each day that first week during our stay in Copenhagen, not that we needed to, of course! "Five-six-seven-eight!" Now we could appreciate all the rehearsals.

We had to be curtain-ready for the rest of our tour: Denmark, Norway, Sweden, Finland, Belgium, France, Holland, and Germany. Copenhagen, the largest city in population, became our home base. We were there three times during the five-month tour, crisscrossing to the other countries at the whim of the public relations people who set the show dates.

On the fourth day in Copenhagen, several of us were having lunch in Giseppe's Italian (a definite no-no because of the healthful diets we were cautioned to follow) when a blonde beauty walked up to the table for autographs. She zoomed in to me first for some reason, a fact for which I soon became grateful.

Because she didn't ask the rest of the Chips for their John Hancocks, I took it as a personal triumph.

After a brief conversation, I gave the Danish girl, Eileen, two complimentary tickets for the show that night and asked her to meet me afterward. She was thankful, even squeezed my arm affectionately before departing the restaurant.

I couldn't get through the rest of my lasagna — something new to me, not to finish a meal. Cody and Ernie, noting my lack of appetite, said I looked flushed. Must have a fever.

It was more than a fever; I had a full-blown case of the flu. I was so out of it by six o'clock that evening that I couldn't possibly go on that night, or even the next two.

Brent, my roomy, moved next door with the other gay guys. He was smart not to expose himself to my coughing curse.

The next day around two p.m., when I was hoping I would die, someone knocked on the hall door. It was probably one of the guys with chicken soup, here to play mother hen. I struggled to the door, wearing only my Calvins.

Lo and behold, it was Eileen, the girl I'd given the comps to the previous day, holding a bouquet of flowers. She had found out backstage why I wasn't in the previous night's show, then talked someone into telling her where we were staying.

She smiled sweetly, handed me the flowers, and

told me I looked sexy as hell. Right! About as sexy as a workout nut who had OD'd in the sauna. I was drowning in sweat. I looked like hell and brimstone, without the brimstone — hair an unwashed mess, fever soaring. All I wanted was for everyone to go away and let me die in peace.

My appearance didn't seem to deter what followed.

As we stood in the doorway a foot apart, she reached out to my naked hairy chest and rubbed the sweat around with her palm before zeroing in to tweak my left nipple with her fingers. The response was immediate. My dick agreed with its rigid cousin to the north, springing to readiness under its own power. After all, it didn't know I had the flu.

In seconds, I'd gone from my deathbed fever to a euphoric sexual one, compromised by a beautiful blonde who had a fetish for my sick body. Desire overcame deathbed wishes quickly.

After closing the door, those Calvins disappeared faster than a dropped coconut. She was instantly on her knees, worshipping those coconuts like no one ever had before or since. Giving head was next on the agenda, apparently her great mission in life.

Here I was, as sick as wilted lettuce, leaning against the wall near the door with a sex-starved Danish licking my hard good Chip lollipop like it might melt any minute.

Afterward, in bed, I found out she was a 22-year-old medical student. I took a couple of pills she guaranteed would make me sleep (I don't know what they were). They worked. When I awoke two hours later, I was lying on my back in a bed soaked with sweat.

The girl was gone.

Did I have a wet dream about this Eileen Nightingale? I thought so until I saw flowers sticking out of a bathroom glass on the dresser. Anyway, I felt better. I don't know if it was sex or pill therapy. Whatever! It worked.

The next couple of days, I had the opportunity to find out how, since Eileen reappeared in the naked flesh each day at two o'clock with her own special remedy for what ailed me. A lollipop workout guaranteed to win cream-of-the-crop honors.

The third day, I had recovered and was back in the show — damn it!

After our first six nights in Copenhagen, I managed on our Sunday off to do some sightseeing with none other than Eileen, my sex-a-thon mate. Imagine! She even liked me when I was well.

Eileen had a body to crave for. That crisp Sunday morning, her true-blonde hair glistened in the sunlight, high cheeks rosy from the cold, slender nose perky as a model on a runway. She walked with a kind of cheerleader march as if she could go into a prance routine at a moment's notice.

Eileen introduced me to smorgasbord brunch and

the best pastry I had ever eaten, along Stroget, a mile-long pedestrian shopping street she claimed to be the longest in Europe.

Afterward, we sauntered along shops filled with Danish design — tinplate and silver, porcelain and ceramic. She helped me pick out a leather jacket, really inexpensive by American standards.

That afternoon we toured Rosenborg Castle, summer residence of the royals, then watched the changing of the Royal Guard as they marched, chins jutting out their helmet straps, down the snow-cleared square in front of Amalienborg, the residence of Queen Margrethe and Prince Henrik. Eileen admitted she had never seen either attraction.

Unfortunately, it was the off-season for Tivoli Gardens and it was closed. She told me proudly that Walt Disney had visited Tivoli before designing his Epcot Center at Walt Disney World in Orlando, Florida.

Eileen told me I would be disappointed when I saw the world-famous statue of Hans Christian Andersen's "The Little Mermaid." She was right. The bronze figure sitting on a slab of granite at the edge of the harbor was no more than child-sized, but beautiful in detail.

I ended up seeing Eileen the next two times the tour came back to Copenhagen, even stayed with her the second time in her spacious flat (she lived alone) instead of the hotel. I had a hard time keeping up with her because we'd screw five or six times during a night, always starting out with her favorite, an expert workout below the belt. My stamina was stretched to the limit. She was insatiable. We graduated to positions I'd never heard of. No cap and gown required. She'd sit, squat, kneel, lean, and lie down with feet in the air. We'd lie toe to head, you name it. She was talented enough to give a circus side show contortionist an inferiority complex.

As for me, I was soon star-ready for porno films.

All of the guys had sex almost every night. The temptation was enormous with girls throwing themselves at the Chips at every turn. There was always a concern about AIDS sweeping the world, though it didn't keep anyone from doing his duty to womankind. To my knowledge, none of the Chips was HIV-positive. Some may have gotten venereal diseases during the tour; if they did, they didn't boast about it. We all used condoms.

Our tour travel entourage consisted of two buses and two 18-wheel semitrailers. The first bus was occupied by Mark Pakin and the cast, though Mark sometimes flew between cities. We named it "Chip-a-hoy." The show leads commandeered the best seats, those in the rear with fold-out tables — privilege of rank, naturally. The rest of us sat forward. The second bus was for the stagehands, wardrobe ladies, and the rest of the crew. Every inch of the two semis was jammed with scenery, props, wardrobe, pyrotechnic equipment, and lights.

The first day on the road, or as it turned out not a road at all, the four vehicles drove to the Copenhagen docks at Kattegat Bay and onto a seagoing ferry. We were heading across the water to Arhus, Jutland, for our next show dates. Jutland was the only part of Denmark attached to the continent of Europe.

I was to discover during this trip that egomania is not just morbid egotism. It's the habit of referencing everything in terms of one's personal interest. We weren't born with it. Most of the guys who had been around the block were big on the stuff stars are inflicted with: selfishness. I soon learned the art from Ernie, Darrell, Larry, and Cody, who became my drinking buddies. We'd sort of huddle together in the after-hours clubs before going our separate ways, depending on who picked up which chick for the rest of the night's entertainment. Even though the four Musketeers were seasoned veterans of the Chippendale circuit, their insecurities showed through in conversations during the wee hours of the mornings. All four, like me, had problems back home from which they'd run away. Dysfunctional situations, insecurities growing up. I was to share most of their intimate details in months to come.

Such ego trips erupted into occasional oral and physical disputes between primates. Tensions arose with so many exhibitionists vying for king-of-the-mountain status all the time. Fights on the bus. Brawls in the hotel rooms, usually instigated after drinking or drug bouts in the wee hours of the morning, over a girl or a guy or an intended or unintended slight.

During our second Arhus show, I was involved in my own backstage scuffle. We were doing three nights in the second largest city in Denmark to standing-room-only audiences.

Just before the start of the Hotel Chippendale scene, Brent, my roommate, arrived late from his bellboy costume change in the dressing room. I was standing in the wings after the end of the "I'll Be There" number. "Get the hell out of the way, Troy," he yelled, shoving me backwards, obviously in a hurry to get on stage. I almost followed him to repeat the honors.

The other Chips rushed by to start the routine. The tension between Brent and me had been building ever since my bathtub fuck-fest that first night in our shared hotel room. Later, after he'd completed his number, I searched Brent out backstage. When I found him standing in the wings, I yelled, "Who the hell do you think you are, shoving me out of the way like that?" When he turned around, I just hit him in the face. I don't really know why I reacted so strongly. I *do* know my reaction was uncalled for.

He hit me back, and then we went at it. I'd never do such a thing today, but back then, egos were tinderboxes of dynamite unneedful of a match to ignite. I thought at the time the fight had nothing to do with his being gay, but I guess it did. All that tension over the possibility of nighttime action possibly instigated by the church-labeled Antichrist in our room had me doing loops. Of course, nothing had ever happened or ever would. It was all my unrealistic but fertile imagination.

After a couple of fists to the solar plexus, the security guards broke us apart. We'd been warned by Mark to protect our face from any kind of injury for the good of the show. We'd both defied that warning with a couple of telltale bruises that would take a couple of days to heal.

My concern over gays was obviously foisted on me by my church. It was not just my baseball-jock, naive thinking. I'd never been around any homos, thinking they were foreign objects, choosing their sexual lot in life — foreign to me at any rate. You know queers, fags. Stupid, right?

During our bus trip from Arhus south to Odense, I saw my first sex videos of live action on the bus VCR — amateur films Ernie had filmed of nightly escapades of the Chips in Copenhagen.

Shit! I couldn't imagine any of the guys wanting the other Chips to witness their naked sweaty bodies in bed and couch action. Should have known! Their livelihood depended on being exhibitionists after all. But this?

"How could you allow that?" I asked Larry. "I mean, letting Ernie film you with it all hanging out?"

Larry laughed. "Why the hell not? We were stoned.

The bitch loved what we were doing. Look at the way Ernie zooms in to the good parts."

He laughed harder. "He'd make a good film director, don't you think?"

I shook my head. No sacred cows with this crew. Farm animals in rut had more privacy. "I can understand his filming it, I suppose, but why do you want your dick on *20/20*?"

"Why not? Something wrong with my dick?" Larry asked, a serious expression on his face.

That broke me up.

In days to come, those two words "Why not?" became the standard response for any question regarding any and all disgusting acts.

Why not, indeed?

The Chippendale calendar has been one of the top-selling calendars in the world for years. Show leads work hard on their taut bodies in gyms, jogging and exercising to tone their muscles to the max. Their physiques must please the eye of photo-shoot cameras.

The locale for photographing the calendar each year varies among exotic tropical spas with a plethora of white sandy beach and ocean for background fill — dream vacation spots, warm and inviting where posing in the all-right weather fits the all-together. Total frontal nudes are not allowed, but naked posteriors get their mooning moments in the sun.

My roommate Brent made the calendar in 1992.

He was paid well for the photos on winter location and was offered several modeling gigs as a result.

Of course, the guys had to "oil" those well-tuned bodies in order to continue as leads in the show. One of the "oil supplements" responsible for those magnificent muscles was steroids.

No one ever mentioned the steroids they were taking, though we talked and laughed constantly about pot and Ecstasy. But steroids? It was a bitter pill to take. It was like this great secret of the universe that no one wanted to share. Though the Chips knew it was dangerous stuff, their desire to be muscular and get their naked bodies chosen for the annual calendars overrode caution.

Roger, one of the leads, confided in me that, after taking them for more than a year, he'd experienced serious adverse effects such as breast enlargement, changes in sex drive, painful erections, and shrinking and inflammation of the balls. Not a pretty picture.

The anabolic steroids did promote body tissue-building processes and reversed destructive tissue-depleting processes. The increase in muscle size and weight gain was partially attributed to increases in sodium and water retention.

One side effect of taking too many of those little pills was loss of scalp hair while promoting its growth all over the body. No problem! Simply shave it off. Every night. In the dressing room. There was enough body hair left in wastebaskets in those dressing rooms to make hair mattresses for all of us. Every day became a bad hair day for those on steroids.

Darrell took so many that his tits started to grow. Because he was a lead stripper, he planned to have an operation to remove the extra flab after this tour ended. What Twiggy wouldn't have given for his dilemma.

I was intent on the scenery as our tour bus continued south through the snow-covered countryside to Odense, famous as the birthplace of Hans Christian Andersen, son of a shoemaker whose fairy tales enchanted the world in the 1800s.

All of a sudden, Rick, one of this year's leads and a contender for the 1994 calendar, started screaming at the top of his lungs, ran down the aisle from the back, and grabbed the black gay guy, Rob, from his seat. Rick started beating the shit out of Rob for no apparent reason. Though the others on the bus seemed to know what was happening, I was flabbergasted.

The other guys pulled Rick off, held his arms, and dragged him to the back of the bus, talking quietly to him, soothing him back to normal. Thank God, Mark Pakin was on the other bus.

"What the hell was that all about?" I asked Larry.

"Roid Rage. He just freaked out, that's all."

The taboo subject had blasted into the open. "Roid Rage? What's that?"

"His hormonal urges are just all fucked up. Took too many steroids, that's all. Makes you want to beat up people."

"That's all? Damn!" I shook my head. "But why did he pick on Rob? He have a homo or race complex or something?"

"Doesn't matter. Something just set him off. Don't worry, he'll come down after awhile. Dan and Bob will stay with him."

The whole episode scared the hell out of me. I'll bet Hans Christian Andersen managed quite well during his career without steroids. I don't know, maybe that's another fairy tale. Right then, I swore I'd never take them.

The two shows went well in Odense. We'd settled down, performing at top form each night. The routine was the same. Rehearsals during the day were now relegated to Mondays only. I was pretty confident in my singing role, even experimenting on stage with my voice. The subtle changes were noticed by the guys. A couple even said "Great, Troy" once in awhile. The words I was accustomed to back in Kirkland at Cafe DaVinci's were long in coming. I couldn't believe the others wouldn't like to have heard similar words of praise now and then. For some reason, they thought such sentiments a kind of weakness. You went on stage, did your thing, went to the after-hours places, got drunk or stoned, and fucked all night. Period, the end!

The first few weeks, I praised guys on their performances when I thought they'd done an exceptional job. All I got was a grunt or two.

Sales of calendars, T-shirts, and such before and after the show hit a new peak in Odense. G-strings, at $12 U.S. a pop, sold out.

Following the last show that night, the leads reaped the benefits of the buying frenzy. We had an organized routine for which the new Chips were paid twenty bucks a night by Mark to take Polaroid pictures of the leads standing with arms draped around shoulders of anxious girls. Each of us was assigned to one lead per night. We'd place the Polaroids in a paper frame and charge the girls the equivalent of $7 U.S. each. The leads would tip us for services rendered that evening. Occasionally, a girl would ask for a picture of me; I gave it to her at no charge.

That particular night, I sold more than a hundred autographs of Ernie. He made $700 U.S. and tipped me seventy of it.

During the tour, many of the girls brought us gifts — shirts they'd ordered with our pictures on them, teddy bears, flowers, and candy. That was cool. I saved some of the stuff, though it never made it back home.

As we headed north back through Arhus to our last Denmark date for awhile, Jutland's industrial city of Alborg, I was having the time of my life, experiencing what I thought it was all about — DBS, and I don't mean Dun and Bradstreet, I mean drugs, booze, and sex in capital letters. Perhaps I'd rue the day, but not today.

7

The fourth week into the tour, our thirty-member cast and crew boarded a Denmark ferry in Frederikshavn to cross Kattegat again. Our bitching about the sub-freezing temperature rivaled that of the Washington, D.C., Parks Department over the crowds at the Million Man March.

Our destination was Gothenburg, Sweden. A heavy snow had fallen the previous day before the temperature plummeted to hell-frozen-over. The ferry made the journey through wind-tossed seas in just over an hour. Not only the seas were tossed; I, like most of the group, lost my breakfast overboard. It was my first experience with seasickness. I hoped it would be my last.

I was told later by one of the stewards on board that the wind had been blowing twenty knots directly down from Norway. It was colder on deck that day than a Dairy Queen Blizzard.

Gothenburg, situated on the broad River Gota, is a city of half a million or so and is Sweden's principal seaport. "Lively" is a synonym for Gothenburg. Our arrival at the Hotel Sven was a repeat of the Faulkner in Copenhagen. Mobs of young women on the street out front screamed their fantasy wishes. The cold had not curtailed their enthusiasm. It had ours. We needed a Swedish police escort to get us into the hotel for a day of sleep. The nausea had passed, but the melody lingered on via nervous bowels singing their own tune.

At that night's performance, we had recovered enough to decide we would live, though some had doubts. Mark Pakin, having weathered the stormy seas, was relentless with theater management, insisting the heat inside the theater be turned up. The temperature outside was below freezing, and our strippers would literally freeze their buns off baring their flesh.

The heat inside became stifling, causing some of the 2,500 screaming females to do a partial strip of their own.

The show went well until the shower scene, the most famous number in the show. I was on stage left beneath a blue spot, singing a song written for the number "The Strength of a Man." The stage was set with five shower stalls of the Hotel Chippendale as seen through open windows, three on a second-floor level, two on the stage floor on each side of the front door. At the start, three leads in a synchronized choreography slowly stripped to their thongs, then naked a couple of pulled Velcro strips later, all to the beat of the music and my lyrics: "Welcome to my life. Tell me what you're seeing there? Can't you see my soul lay bare and naked at your feet. . . ."

Only their thongs were at their feet, and it wasn't their souls that lay bare. Next they stepped into separate shower stalls, poured liquid soap from plastic bottles into their palms exactly the same way, then soaped up, making sure to make important body parts shine in the spotlights. The girls whistled appropriately, stood, and started to stamp their feet like football fans in a grandstand doing the stampede bit.

"There's nothing else to hide. Just pure emotion. Never can decide. I have to give, just like air I breathe is such a part of me forever. . . ."

Although naked, the leads made sure their movements prevented frontal nudity from audience view, regardless of the explicit yells, which were especially raunchy tonight. The next step was to shower, dry off, then slowly dress, then blackout for the next scene.

Oops! Double oops! After soaping up, the boys reached in unison to the shower faucets attached to European-style bathtub hoses. They turned the faucets clockwise. No water. Not a drip on a Chip. The prop man, who had quit the previous night over a salary dispute, had failed to refill the stage prop water tanks, no doubt on purpose.

I heard a couple of stage moans and jerked my head around. The guys held the nozzles against their arms waiting for someone to turn on the water. Then I noticed their unbelieving stares at the shower heads.

What do three naked Chippendales do, all soaped up and nowhere to rinse? They grin and bare it.

I could only continue singing.

Somehow, the boys decided in unison to gather their suds where they may and pretend to wash them off. By now, they were all giggling, nodding at one another, sliding hands down slippery legs to remove some of the offending bubbly onto the prop floor.

The Chips were at least back in sync again, reaching for their bath towels on the shower stall racks. Whups! No towels!

The replacement for Henry, the absent prop hand, was finished as a towel boy.

The guys discovered the lack of terry at the same time, soapy rears mooning the audience in rhythm. I sang on, barely suppressing laughter at three slick Chips wishing they hadn't been so enthusiastic with their soap.

The shower stall floors were obviously slippery as hell now, causing the men to slip and slide in unplanned rhythm. One cannot cry over spilled soap; neither can a nude Chippendale. The synchronization was history, as the Chips, looking like Tonya Harding on ice with her skates untied, reached clumsily for different colored golf shirts. They looked at one another, teased the shirts over their slick and sticky nude bodies, while keeping themselves from falling down — a stitch in time, all the way to the finale. With a jacket thrown over one shoulder and a sick smile at the audience, the images disappeared in a blackout.

So much for a shower. Water over the man.

Though I was still queasy from the seasickness and had forgone dinner, I pranced gamely on stage following the shower scene to perform my big solo number, "I'll Be There." I couldn't help notice a couple of young women in the front row with their nipples literally poking out of cut-out holes in their leather bras. My God! Who was supposed to be doing the strip here?

I almost lost my cool, but kept singing, even staying on key. "I'll be there, I'll be there, just call my name and I'll be there. . . ."

The ladies started clapping to the beat, then standing and stamping their feet on the wooden theater floor again. Frenzy took on new meaning as I looked into sweaty faces in the first few rows. In sympathy, I started to perspire. No. Truthfully, it was from a sudden fear tickling my spine. I wasn't quite sure why, but something seemed amiss. The natives were getting restless. Too restless!

I started the chorus nervously. "Just look over your shoulder, baby. . . ."

The next thing I knew, thirty or so women were coming up the stairs on each side of the stage. I jerked my head like a tennis match spectator, side to side, hoping someone in the wings could see what the hell was happening. Still, I continued to sing into the hand-mike, when I should have been screaming for help. Surely these women wouldn't do anything drastic?

Wrong!

In the next minute, they rushed, a cattle stampede as destructive as any you've ever witnessed in a John Wayne western. "Out of control" were the operative words for that frantic crowd.

What does one do in a stampede?

You duck your head, then panic. The first couple of seconds, this physical adoration was funny. Funny became serious faster than a coed getting knifed in a horror movie. I lost my mike into greedy hands, then my clothes, a piece at a time. They ripped my shirt right off, then tore my T-shirt into shreds. Fingernails were scraping my chest and back. The shrill screams were so deafening I couldn't hear my heart thumping distress signals.

The remaining audience was on their feet going ape-shit at this impromptu strip scene, cheering on their peers to pull at my belt and whatever else they could get their hands on. Nimble fingers cupped my crotch and ass, fighting for a feel. The music demanded more, creating a frenzy of its own. I was down to my Calvin Kleins and boots before you could say "Gypsy Rose Lee."

I became scared out of my gourd when I realized a second later that I was going to suffocate. Despite their being over me like Winnie-the-Pooh after honey, I fought back, striking out with doubled fists and connecting with a couple of jaws.

I was down for the count, or the countess as it were, for one woman was on top of me humping for all the world against my Calvins. A hand scraped down my side, caught the underwear band, and ripped it down.

I thought my nuts were on the way to storage for the winter as another hand grabbed them and squeezed like they were her personal property. I clamped my eyes shut and did my own screaming.

Suddenly, I felt weight lifting off me, female bodies parting like Moses's sea. I was pulled into a sitting position, then erect, facing the audience.

The cavalry had arrived and none too soon. Security, in the impressive form of three of our strongest bodyguards, was manhandling the screeching females off the stage by the numbers.

If this scene hadn't gotten so serious, it would have been hilarious. The audience took the latter view, pointing, whistling in a most unladylike way, and yelling obscenities that would have embarrassed Howard Stern.

Now, not only my soul lay bared to the world. The security boys, in their overdue haste to vanquish the Swedish conquerors, failed to retrieve my clothes, now Chip souvenirs of doubtful worth. Because they had not had time to bring a robe or towel with them, I made my dash to freedom in my birthday suit without so much as a candle to blow out.

For a week following, I looked like Peter Cottontail fresh from the briar patch. Thank God, I didn't have to strip during the show. My scratched body might have provoked another attack. Needless to say, throughout the rest of the tour, I was careful during the "I'll Be There" number, all alone on the stage, eyes darting to the steps now and again, ready to run at any sign of a stampede.

Oddly enough, TV Sweden was in the theater that night, filming a segment for a *60 Minutes*-type show on the Chippendale phenomenon engulfing Europe. My unexpected disrobing made the TV network news all over Sweden.

I had my moment of fame. Sensational though it was, my streaking across the stage stark naked and bleeding after the assault was tame stuff for Swedish television. Male or female frontal nudity is even allowed on the six o'clock news. I hoped at least the incident in Sweden might boost my career.

No such luck! I was an anonymous Chippendale (they hadn't bothered to use my name) performing sans clothes.

Had I visited a tanning salon before my nude debut, I might have been better received by the Swedish press. Yes, the local *Gothenburg Post* referred to me as that "pretty American, male, pale and white as a sail." You can't win!

I tried to get a video copy of that show for a souvenir of the wonderful city of Gothenburg, but the local station wouldn't release it. At least the incident gave the rest of the cast something for which to poke fun at me for the rest of the week. Fortunately, instant fame is as fleeting as a sail in a windstorm.

8

The April weather lessened its death grip on winter. Temperatures cooperated, warming enough to allow snow to start its spring meltdown on Gothenburg streets. I felt better too, no longer looking like a tom-cat after a bad night on the fence.

The Saturday night choice of an after-show-hours club, as proclaimed from the stage by Ernie, was a rave club. My first. I'd heard about them from the other guys of course, but hadn't actually been to one. Such a showtime announcement assured local clubs of a late turnout of women. Part of the bargain was no expensive cover charges and free drinks for the Chips during the wee hours of the morning.

Rave clubs are actually Ecstasy clubs — disco bars of the Nineties if you will — with the added feature of those little acid-like pills called "the love drug." The dope is a modern-day version of MDA of the Sixties.

Naturally, the eight of us were exempt from the club's cover charge, a hefty $35 U.S. a pop. Even the water, dispensed at $5 a bottle, was free to us. Water? It's the drink of choice in a rave club. Has something to do with all the hot dancing and the effects of Ecstasy on the body.

The disco music bombarded us as we entered, blasting away so loud that Beethoven could have heard it. It was impossible to be understood without shouting.

Pulsing strobe lights added a neon-hiccup look to the dance floor. Spinning revelers fought for enough space to breathe. Choking cigarette smoke drifted aimlessly about as if an overzealous nicotine-dispensing steam engine was attached to the heating system. I quickly realized there was no pot odor. My astuteness sometimes amazes me!

It took a couple of minutes for my eyes to adjust to the darkness.

Many of the night advocates wore rave-type clothing, everything from jeans to cutoffs to slinky dresses. Wild spiked hair in fuchsia and purple was the norm. And everything was pierced with rings: nipples, noses, ears, tongues, lips, eyebrows, probably a few other things only intimacy would reveal. And leather! Enough to satisfy Fonda on a Honda.

It was hard to tell the males from the females, not that it mattered.

A short white guy about my age wearing an expensive black leather jumpsuit, sidled up to me and grabbed a sore elbow. "I'm Doc Holiday. Want some juice?" A ring wrestled with his nostrils and lips over territorial rights. His words were European-accented.

I thought they only served water here. "No, I don't—"

"Ecstasy, man," Doc said, baring his pearlies. "Turn you on . . . make you love eve-ry-body."

"Oh. Yeah?" I glanced at my buddy, Cody, unsure. Somehow I didn't think Wyatt Earp's best friend started out in Tombstone this way.

Cody pushed a comb through short black hair, then laid his slender fingers on my shoulder.

"Ecstasy's the deal for the night, Troy. Doc Holiday's right. Makes you love eve-ry-body. One little pill will keep you high a good six hours." Cody never let his Jewish Orthodox background keep him from the hard stuff, which he consumed in ever-increasing quantities. "Come on, man. Do you good. Shouldn't be here if you're not going to get with the program."

I'd never tried the stuff, was actually afraid to. But Cody was putting my head in a mind-wrestle. Wanted to stay. I put on a happy face. "Six hours you say? Damn! Sounds like my kind of medicine. How much, Holiday?"

"That's Doc, Chip. Hundred twenty-five kroner . . . twenty-five U.S."

"Hell!" I shouted. "I don't want to buy the farm?"

"Gotta bunch of sick mouths to feed, Mr. Chippendale. And they're all awaiting prescriptions from the

Doc." He laughed, then gave me a serious shit-or-get-your-own-pot look. "You in or out, dude?"

I turned on my most knowing smile. "How many for a hundred twenty-five kroner?"

He stared, then shouted above the din, "You Polish or something?"

"American," I said with a straight face.

Doc Holiday looked at the laughing Cody, then back at me. "You fuckin' with me, dude?"

"No."

"One."

"Okay. Okay." I pulled out enough kroner to satisfy the Doc for two of the peas in pods. Might as well double my pleasure, double my fun. After all, it was my virgin trip into this surreal world of rock and funk.

Doc Holiday pulled out a sequined Ziploc bag and doled out two pills filled with God-knows-what.

After the good Doctor had moved on to the other Chips, sickies all, Darrell came over. He nodded at Doc Holiday, "Dope dicks pay big time to get exclusive dealer nights in these clubs."

"No shit, Sherlock! I didn't know drugs were legal in Sweden."

"They're not. But nobody cares."

The next day, I was told that Ecstasy was dangerous medicine. Dancers high on the stuff who drank too much water in a rave club would sometimes keel over. Some had been known to die of overdoses. It was bad shit all right, adversely affecting the heart.

Everybody on the floor was in a Saturday night fever, making John Travolta look like an amateur. I grabbed a bottle of water and downed my two pills. Nothing! No reaction. Maybe it took awhile to take effect. The music enticed my body onto the dance floor. The beat hammered my libido like a whip in the hands of Indiana Jones. No music breaks for the weary. Dance till you drop was the bombastic message, loud and clear.

After ten minutes or so of communal dancing, I headed toward the back booths and men's room for a piss break.

Oops! Not everyone here was dancing, unless you consider humping like Pekingese dancing. I later discovered some of the girls in leather had slits in their pants at a very appropriate place. The guys would just unzip and fuck away fully clothed.

The bathrooms reconfirmed my observations. Television scenes of New Orleans at Mardi Gras came to mind. There were no men's and women's signs on the doors, just "Water Closet." The mixed crowd wasn't there for water or even bladder relief. People were fucking in the stalls, open doors a personal invitation to the orgy.

I had to fight my way to the urinal. Naturally, that's when the Ecstasy drifting through my body decided to put out the welcome mat. All I could do was smile as I relieved myself. One minute I was sober, the next suddenly woozy and reeling. I reached out to a guy's arm standing at the next urinal to steady myself. The person obviously didn't resent the intrusion or he would have smacked me one in the jaw. Apparently the guy was in as bad a shape as myself, because he held onto my arm while we emptied our bladders.

My head was whirling now. I started laughing as I zipped up. I think I zipped up. I pushed my way through the leather tundra to the hall door. Gotta get back to that beat. Gotta dance . . . gotta dance! Everybody was suddenly my friend, laughing, holding hands, hugging — men with men, women with women, men with women, whatever. I think there was a big dog in there somewhere. This love drug was cool stuff.

Nothing seemed to matter anymore, other than to cling onto somebody, anybody, moving or standing still on the dance floor or off. It was like a never-never land stuffed with fun-loving gypsies without a tambourine in sight, bent on giving and receiving ultimate pleasure. Unbelievably, it wasn't a sexual high for me, just a loving high.

Suddenly, about two a.m., whistles started blasting everywhere around me. The music stopped. Strange popping sounds imitating small firecrackers exploding broke the quiet. It took a few seconds to realize everyone was throwing pills onto the dance floor and backing away to the benches surrounding it.

My God! It was a police raid. Darrell had said that nobody cared about all the drugs. Wrong! The Gothenburg police cared.

What shitty luck! My first rave club, my first Ecstasy

pills, and a damned raid. I followed everyone else's lead and sat on a bench. Everything seemed hilarious, like a scene in a slapstick comedy. Stupid, and hilarious!

The lights turned up to stage bright. The decor that had seemed subtle and sexy before was now like a Christmas tree turned on in the daylight, garish and ugly.

The party was over, and I was just getting started with this Ecstasy thrill. It owed me another five hours of bliss.

If I hadn't been so strung out, I would have been terrified of getting arrested.

Cody, Ernie, and Darrell found their way over and sat next to me, soon to be followed by the other Chips. It was a safety in numbers sort of thing, a fact I appreciated even in my drugged state. We were sticking together, just a few good men having a good time. We were innocent, just came here because we were invited, got caught up in the festivities, that's all. Let's face it, we were celebrities. Chippendale men all. They couldn't arrest celebrities, could they?

The ten or so policemen, swinging wooden clubs threateningly, began searching each person. I couldn't for the life of me figure out why they were bothering. The Ecstasy pills littered the damned floor in fuckin' plain sight. All they had to do was scoop them up.

All of a sudden I felt inspired. Sudden mood shifts, such as from despair to elation, were one of the peculiarities of Ecstasy. I started singing the nonsensical lyrics to "The Lion Sleeps Tonight." After a couple of "A-wimowehs," everyone in the place, except the police, joined in.

"In the jungle, the mighty jungle, the lion sleeps tonight. . . ." Soon I was standing like a choir director, leading the Ecstasy enthusiasts, waving my arms to my inspired rhythm, whatever that was. "A-wimoweh, a-wimoweh."

At that moment, I spotted an attractive woman across the dance floor. She was a lioness and she wasn't sleeping. While the police continued to search the 300 or so punkers, I made my way across to the smiling feline with a blonde mane to die for.

Without so much as another "A-wimoweh," I started laying big sloppy kisses on her. She responded with tongue-like ambition. When I pulled myself away from her luscious lips, I started sweet-talking her like she was the only woman on earth and I was the only man who had ever fallen in love. I have no idea what I said or what she said, but it didn't seem to matter. We were in love at that moment, in that place, standing in the bright lights of the rave club with policemen surrounding us shouting Gestapo-like orders to everyone.

Bizarre with a capital "B."

Reality finally hit home when a policeman pulled me away from the Swedish woman and asked for my passport. Thank God, I had it with me.

By now, the night revelers were thinning out. Each person, after showing ID or passport and being body-searched, was being ushered out the front door, not arrested.

They were actually searching for Doc Holiday, the long-gone Ecstasy pusher in the leather jumpsuit.

One problem remained. Ernie nudged me. "Shit, I don't have my passport. It's back at the hotel!" Ernie was a Chippendale lead with a muscular body he loved to love, midnight black hair down to his abs, and Roman-chiseled cheeks that had graced several Chippendale calendars. He had become my best friend on the tour, at least I thought of him that way. We palled around together. Perhaps it had something to do with our mutual interest in music and singing. He definitely had an ego problem (didn't we all), expecting everyone to kowtow to his whims, no matter how strange. They usually did.

So did I. I played the high Samaritan. Gave up my lioness and volunteered to go back to the hotel for Ernie's passport. In an emergency, Ernie would have done the same for me.

When I returned to the rave club with the forgotten travel document, everyone was gone but Ernie and two policemen. The attractive girl had escaped into the night.

So ended my first experience at a rave club, still high on Ecstasy and without a lioness to share my den.

Oddly enough, I received a love letter and picture from the mystery woman the next day. She'd left the envelope at the hotel desk with my name on it. No return address. I wondered how she knew my name until Ernie told me he'd given it to her while I was fetching his passport. It was really a touching letter, filled with remarks about true love and how it was too bad we hadn't had the chance to do more than kiss and hug. Of course, I was so high on Ecstasy, I would have sweet-talked one of the cops. I couldn't even remember what she looked like. The photo helped.

I felt a twinge of guilt over the entire episode. What would my strict religious parents think of their darling son, sitting in a Gothenburg jail having gotten busted for drugs?

It was the first and last time I tried Ecstasy. Lack of control and memory scared the shit out of me. I wouldn't try it again on a bet.

9

It was a clear Wednesday evening in Gama Stan, the Old Town section of Stockholm, Sweden, our next stop on the tour.

Gama Stan, a downtown island saddled with a maze of narrow cobblestone alleys, was filled with antique shops, art boutiques, pubs, and restaurants, dominated by the massive eighteenth-century Royal Palace crowning its western extremity.

This far north in Sweden the midnight air was stinging crisp, wind sharp enough to steal your breath. Drifts from the previous weekend's snowfall were tire-deep. Old Town snowplows had done their damnedest to clear the curving pedestrian street, Vasterlanggatan, leaving frozen slush piled along the curbs, a Mr. Winter smile jammed with dirty teeth.

Ancient buildings restored to their original splendor clutched one another with common walls, proud of their four-floor facades flaunting the history of this beautiful part of Stockholm, a city known throughout the world for its annual Nobel Prize award ceremonies held at the Stadshuset a few blocks away.

At midnight, the shops had closed for the day, leaving tourists and revelers a no-nonsense choice of late-night attractions in which to spend their kroner. These restaurants, pubs, and nightclubs elbowed their way between shops lining the promenade where royalty and commoners had strolled for 300 years.

Twelve of us muscular, lean-machine Chippendale dancers crunched through the snow along Vasterlang-gatan in our leather boots, talking and laughing about the performance that evening at the Regina Theater a few blocks over behind the famous Strand Hotel (unfortunately, we weren't staying there, not at $425 a night, thank you). Trailing behind were a couple of Chippendale security — bouncer types — hired to protect us from jealous husbands and boyfriends who might take exception to our allure to women and be lurking in the dark alleyways.

Earlier that evening, I was astounded as usual by the 3,500 or so females threatening to bring down the gilded, ornate ceiling of the Stockholm Theater with their screaming. The awesome noise was a tidal wave of adoration washing toward the stage, making me feel like I was on top of the world.

Ernie, Larry, Darrell, and Cody were in the group as we strolled down the snowy sidewalk. We five lived for the parties and sex. That's what I'd discovered the tour was all about thus far, hadn't I? Parties and sex! It wasn't just a well-paying show business opportunity to further my singing career, including an all-expenses-paid tour of European cities and hot nightclubs.

Up ahead, the long line of women shifting their feet in the snow to keep the blood circulating told me we'd arrived at the pre-ordained, after-hours hot spot for tonight, Café Opera.

As we approached the club, the screams started as if we'd taken off our bikinis instead of our jackets. We were here in the flesh, so to speak. We were on a snowy, icy stage, strutting our stuff in the frigid air, T-shirts bulging in the right places. After all, body beautifuls were expected.

The Café Opera bouncer motioned us to the front of the line and quickly ushered us inside. We expected nothing less. The female adoration in the hinterlands erupted like the crowd at a Rocky Balboa fight.

Welcome to the party!

The room was filled with young, beautiful, shapely women; some not so young, beautiful, or shapely; some stringy-looking with punk haircuts and a plethora of rings jutting from orifices; boobs oozing out the tops of short dresses; tantalizing female asses filling leather pants tight enough for Madonna. Most of them were here to welcome the Chips.

Café Opera was a beautiful three-story night-club with high ceilings, an elegant and sophisticated atmosphere filled with crystal sconces and flocked red wallpaper, many steps above our usual evening haunts. A noisy casino jammed with smitten roulette players lingered enticingly across the lower floor. I expected to see James Bond sitting at a baccarat table. All that was missing were the gowns, tuxedos, and dry vodka martinis shaken, not stirred.

The smoke cloud lay heavy and rude about us. One sniff of marijuana aroma was enough to tell me we were in the right place at the right time.

By now, I'd learned to pace myself, not to choose the first girl who appealed to me as the night's sex partner. I still had a lot of partying to do. Besides, something better might come along.

I moved around, drinking and smoking a joint, and schmoozed with the good-looking women, most of whom were openly receptive to a turn in my hotel bedroom.

As the wee hours dwindled, I hadn't found Miss Right for the night. It was nearly four a.m. when a gorgeous blonde joined me. She had a body so curvaceous that a teenaged boy might have drawn it. I don't remember exactly what she said to get my attention, maybe it was just a touch on the shoulder, but her next comment in perfect English did. "Let's go back to your hotel room and fuck like crazy." Magical words sure to get a response. I felt a tingle in the lower regions.

She was beautiful — and young. I knew after a few minutes' conversation that she was a tryout reject from

Born Yesterday, really naive and not too bright, but sexier than all hell with tits bouncing, threatening to burst the threads of her snug pink sweater. She had the brightest blue eyes this side of Elizabeth Taylor, typical of Swedish women, and blonde locks that spilled to smooth shoulders.

Hello, Miss Right!

About that time, most of the Chips decided to head back to the Diplomat Hotel. I was more than ready. A couple of the guys had picked out mates for the chamber, and I had mine beside me, Christina, looking delicious enough to eat.

As we headed down the icy sidewalk of Vasterlanggatan, I nudged Ernie. "Can I use your room for the babe? Brent and I have this agreement. I don't bring women to our room, he doesn't bring men, unless we make prior arrangements. There's nothing prior about four in the a.m.!"

Ernie smiled and put his arm around my shoulders. "Only if you share the blonde with me."

Whoops! That shook me. I'd never done that kind of thing before, a three-way, I mean. Was this a homo type of thing? Right off, the idea made me nervous as hell. Ernie's straight, isn't he? He's one of the leads in the show stripping nude all the time, showing off his body, and. . . .

"What's the matter? You going chickenshit on me?"

"No. It's just that, I've never—" I stopped myself from exposing my naiveté. Hell, this was just sex —

tea for three, that's all. Besides, I was pretty wasted by then. "Sure! Let's do it, man. Why not?"

So ten minutes later, Ernie, Christina, and I were in his Diplomat Hotel room choked with blue-striped wallpaper and turret-like molding bordering the ceiling. Mirrors glared back as though Ernie had arranged them to reflect the action emanating from a four-poster bed any Swedish king would cherish.

I made small talk as I circled Christina's wagon, prepping for the attack, while Ernie tuned the nightstand clock radio to rock and roll. After turning all the lights on to star bright, he started removing his clothes. Christina beat him to it, dropping her minidress to the floor quicker than a Chippendale strip, leaving her naked as a Blue Lagoon swimmer, moaning, "Hurry up. I want to feel a hard Chippendale inside me."

Ernie was naked and ready in a nanosecond, kneeling on the rug in front of her, holding his erection, telling her roughly, "Get down here and suck me off."

Funny! I thought she was my date.

I wasn't quite used to this cavalier approach to sex. No foreplay. Just a "suck me off" from another guy in the room with a demanding tool and no work permit.

She wasn't concerned about foreplay, so why should I be? They just hadn't taught me the Queensberry Rules of sex in Wenatchee Bible School. "Should I be doing this?" thoughts entered my mind, then vanished in a flash of desire.

She dropped to the floor on all fours, obviously

knowing her way around an erection, taking Ernie all the way on first gulp.

Her nudeness, bent over like a bitch in heat, was hot stuff for a small-town boy. There was no doubt she was a true blonde.

I was bare to the skin before an umpire could holler "Strike" and standing behind her ready to do my best with a limp bat — a back-door entry, my only choice at the moment.

Problem time — I couldn't get hard. That had never happened to me before!

I stood there, fondling myself, trying to get erect enough to baptize myself in a condom. No luck! I knew the reason was the stiff competition up front. The image didn't quite jibe with my earlier plan. One-on-one sex with Miss Right had gone wrong for the evening.

Christina mumbled between tongue licks, "You having trouble back there, Troy?"

I must have turned fifteen shades of red, even as drunk as I was. "Shit no!" Hell, she was questioning my manly prowess. I tried a mindset of other sexual situations, doing it with other women on tour thus far. Nothing! Finally, I thought about me on the receiving end of Christina's sultry mouth. That did it. I rose to the occasion. I was now hard enough to start batting practice. I rolled on the condom and, without preliminary, shoved it in from the rear and started to ride. Amazing! She was ambidextrous, rotating her shapely ass, while still sucking Ernie like a Hoover.

The windows of the room were fogged over. I don't know if it was from the cold outside or the heat inside. Even with all the steamy action, I couldn't get off. The stimulation wasn't there. I really wasn't into trio flights. Duos were my thing. Female and male duos, one of each. Maybe it was the lack of attention from Christina. She was more concerned with satisfying Ernie than me. What happened to "Let's go back to your hotel room and fuck like crazy?" Moral: Don't invite another Chip to the party!

Maybe if it had been two women instead of two men, the ménage-à-Troy might have worked for me. I was to find my way into one of those later in the tour.

I sighed, pulled out, peeled off the rubber, dropped it on the rug, and flopped into a chair. I watched Christina vacuuming Ernie. I don't think she even realized I was no longer pumping her from behind. The scene became boring. Ridiculous, but still boring. The voyeur bit wasn't my Valhalla either.

I pulled on jeans and a Chippendale T-shirt with my picture emblazoned on the front and walked out into the hall barefoot. Larry and Darrell were lounging against the wall, passing back and forth a bottle of vodka they'd snitched from the courtesy bar in the hotel lobby. It wasn't as though well-paid Chips couldn't afford to buy liquor; it was just more fun to swipe it.

Larry was the muscular Chip who did the "Breakfast in Bed" solo fucking number at center stage during the show. His wavy, dirty-blond, shoulder-length hair bounced as he did push-ups on a stage bed, totally alone and naked during his big number. He simulated a climax, adding a toothy smile, lit up a cigarette, and blew a perfect smoke ring. To the delight of squealing women in the audience, he added, "I had a great time. Call me."

I asked as a joke, "You guys wanna have sex?"

Darrell spat out in a deep voice, "We're into girls, honey."

Their laughter awakened half the floor, no doubt.

"No, no, you assholes, I meant Ernie's in his room getting a fantastic blowjob from this Swedish slut. She's a knockout with her mouth, so Ernie says."

Without skipping a beat, Larry said, "Ernie moans. He don't talk when a slut is suckin'."

"Okay. So he moans like she's a knockout with her mouth. That good enough?"

Darrell said, "Good with a capital G. Lead on, Mr. Kline. We're your men."

No . . . no, I started to say. I was just kidding around. I didn't actually mean for them to join in.

The next thing I knew, Darrell and Larry entered the room. I reluctantly followed and shut the door. What was I getting myself into? The sights and clamor inside were sexier than a fuck video. Ernie was sounding like his pumping engine was about to blast off. Christina was still on the rug on all fours, face flushed, body slick with sweat, sucking away. She was as wet as a seal fresh out of the Baltic Sea. Women aren't supposed to sweat, are they?

Larry watched them a second, then said to me in a low voice filled with disgust, "What a dirty fuckin' bitch." He growled, then chuckled. "I love dirty fuckin' bitches!"

First thing I knew, he'd pulled out a condom, slipped it on his forefinger, bent over, and started sliding it in and out of her. I wondered, How in hell does a guy get a disease from a finger in there? I was as embarrassed as all hell by this situation, but couldn't let these macho guys know it.

Larry was the type who had a kaleidoscope of sex with countless women day and night. Had something to do with his dumber-than-dumb look and manner. Always made out when others failed. He was into diversions I never dreamed of — or so he boasted. He was making a believer out of me tonight.

About this time, all the weird action hit me. I mean, the scene was so wild it was surreal. Ernie was pumping his bike to the finish line while Larry pedal-fucked Christina from behind, intent on giving her the ride of her life.

In my wildest imagination, I could never have pictured myself in this erotic scene with four Jacks and a Jill and not a hill in sight. Though I felt totally mortified and ashamed to be a part of it all, I couldn't stop watching.

Christina was really into it. There was no "I can't

do that, or I won't do this." It was "I can't believe I'm with the Chippendales." That's so sick, I mean with guys using her as a sex toy, degrading her in every way.

Little did I know, the scene was going to get even more bizarre.

Ernie finally got his nut. He patted her cheeks to let go of him. She groaned as he pulled out. So did he.

Without straightening, Christina moaned, between gasps, "Hot . . . enough, Mr. Chippendale?" After all, Larry was moving into overdrive from behind with his rubber-clad twinkie, trying for a personal best, or at the very least a gold medal in finger-fucking.

Ernie said, "Fantastic, baby. You're good enough to be a star in a porno movie."

Larry plunged his digit faster than a piston, until she yelled her orgasmic pleasure. He pulled out the slimy finger and licked it clean before peeling off the condom. "Tastes like strawberries. You been stuffin' strawberries in there, honey?"

Yuk! Disgusting.

Darrell had that glazed look in his eyes. He was naked with an erection as hard as a barber pole and pushing Christina onto her back before Larry could get his jeans unbuckled. Sweaty Christina was a Cinderella ready for another slipper. Her prince had arrived, dreams coming true assured. She was down for the Chips again.

Darrell was soon fucking away, oblivious to rowdy

spectators cheering him on, for the first few minutes anyway.

This bit of absurd staging set me off. I burst into hysterical laugher, ignoring my previous hesitancy to be a part of this show.

Christina got pissed over my antics. "Are you making . . . fun of me?" she stuttered between lunges of Darrell's body slamming his missile home.

I laughed harder.

By now, Darrell was getting pissed, too. I was interrupting his rhythm. That was all he ever talked about during dance rehearsals — "Got to get the rhythm just right; rhythm is everything!"

"Get the hell out of here, you guys." Apparently he, like me, preferred fucking without voyeurs or extraneous rumblings to alter his "rhythm."

The three of us stood in the small bathroom, drinking Larry's vodka and making rude remarks. I still had my clothes on. Larry did, too. Playing with her nether regions with only a tether finger did not require nudity. Ernie was still naked, temporarily drained from her undressed rehearsal manipulations.

Larry pulled a joint from his shirt pocket. In a few minutes, the antics in the bedroom took on the dimensions of a *Candid Camera* episode. I should have stayed in the bathroom.

Later, back in Ernie's bedroom, after Darrell was through filling her with Chip charisma, Christina, the other Chips, and I sat around drinking the rest of the vodka and sharing another joint. Christina was lying on the bed, still naked as Eve in search of an apple, sweat rolling between her heaving breasts. She had given Ernie the blowjob of a lifetime while being pumped from behind by me, then finger-fucked by Larry, followed by a prize-winning screw by the tap-dancing dick of Darrell.

My mind was reeling, and not just from the pot and vodka. I was humiliated, yet I was still there condoning every action. She was so dumb, so vulnerable. And she didn't care, lying there naked, head on a pillow, continuing to moan, "I can't believe I'm fuckin' around with the Chippendales."

In her next breath, she was saying, "I want to go to Hollywood and be a star." She'd picked up on what Ernie had said earlier. "Can you guys get me into the movies?"

Darrell cracked, "Yeah, sure. Free, too. There's one just down the street."

That broke us up again.

Ernie sobered first. "Yeah, Christina, you'd make a terrific porn star in America."

"You really think so?" I swear her nipples stood at attention.

Darrell said, "Yeah, sure. Young, good-looking chick like you. How old are you anyway?"

"Eighteen."

Darrell quipped, "Perfect." He fingered his Kirk

Douglas chin. "But there's just one thing wrong with this picture."

Christina sat up, looking hurt, tits jiggling. Her lower lip curved into a pout. "What's that?"

"All the women in America shave below."

I cut my laugh short when Darrell flashed me a dirty look.

"You're kidding, aren't you?" Christina asked, shaking her pretty head.

Darrell added, "No, it's true. You can't be an American porno star unless you're smooth as a peach." He winked at Larry.

She thought that one over, still pouty, then brightened.

"I can fix that. I like peaches. Anybody got a razor?"

Larry broke in. "No. Gotta be done by a professional barber." Sounded like a hair-raising experience to me.

"Really?" It was her favorite word.

Larry added, "Yeah. Used to shave women for a livin' before I joined up with the Chips. Worked for a buncha porno film directors. I'm a hair stylist, ain't I, Darrell?"

"Shit, yeah, baby. He's a regular Edward Scissorhands!"

Wait a minute, that was my profession before I joined the Chips. Of course, the son of a bitch, Larry, was a lying Pinocchio, only it wasn't his nose that was getting longer.

"If you're sure. Okay. Why not?" She rubbed a finger between her legs. "I want to be more American."

So Ernie got his shaving shit from the bathroom, laid a towel over the sheet, and helped Christina reposition herself with legs bent at the knees, pubic bush open for public viewing as if it were sidewalk art.

Larry lathered her up with his fingers, sans condom, spending more time than necessary for a little lather, even poking some inside as a reserve. "Adding some cream to those strawberries, honey."

This scene was too much! Awesome! Larry bent over Christina, shaving her twat, an obvious lump threatening to break the zipper of his jeans, and Ernie, Darrell, and I watching as though this were the Second Coming. No doubt it soon would be.

When Larry finished, Darrell joined in, "Yeah, baby. You look sexier than Vanessa Del Rio."

She lay there bald as a baby's butt, grinning ear to ear. "Give me that joint." She took a couple of tokes, then smoothed herself seductively, turning herself on again. Everyone else, too!

"Anybody for seconds?

Ernie giggled, "She's peachy keen and ready."

Darrell laughed. "Sure, but wait a minute, Ernie. How adventurous are you, Christina?"

She looked wary for a minute, took another puff on the joint, allowing the smoke to curl seductively out of her nose, and said wheezily, "How much more adventurous can I get, baby?"

Darrell smiled. "I've always had this kind of fantasy!"

Uh-oh! I thought. What now?

She said, "What kind of fantasy?"

Darrell said, "I've always wanted to piss on a naked girl."

"Really?"

I choked on the joint and started coughing.

"Yeah."

"Where?"

"All over." Darrell laughed Eddie Murphy-like.

"Let's do it in the bathroom," he said, pulling her into a sitting position. "You can lie down in the tub. We can all piss on you.

"It's called a golden shower," he added, as if he'd just heard the term for the first time.

I stopped laughing. This had gotten way out of hand. This suggestion was so degrading that I couldn't take any more. The four-way and shaving incident had already been wilder than any circus sideshow act, but I could have left at any time. I hadn't.

I did this time.

I reminded myself that I wasn't at their point of sexual deviancy. This was my virgin tour. They'd been Chips for several years and had been involved in every situation and done absolutely everything. They obviously had no respect for women or themselves.

I can't say I had had too much at that point either, because otherwise I wouldn't have stayed in that room with all the degrading shit going on, condoning it by doing nothing to prevent it.

I got the hell out of the room. Never should have stayed in the first place.

The next day, I felt so humiliated about what I'd done and witnessed that I didn't ask any of the guys how the evening had ended with my date. I was over the line now — way over the line of degradation.

10

The first of May, having spent the previous two weeks in Stockholm doing ten sold-out shows, we rode the buses to Oslo, the capital of Norway. Clustered around the head of Oslofjord, Oslo is reputed to be the most spacious city in the world. Everyone seems to have a bit of frozen paradise. The deep harbor probed right into the heart of the city, allowing cruise ships to disperse tourist passengers during the summer season. Ferries serviced Copenhagen and Frederikshavn, Denmark, from the same docks.

We arrived early afternoon at the Ambassadeur Hotel, an edifice in the style of New Orleans' French Quarter, a pale pink facade accented with wrought iron balconies. The next day was free, a reprieve from the strenuous rehearsals, matinees, and evening shows in Stockholm. Although the others mostly slept the day away, I did the tourist bit alone, starting with a stop in the hotel gift shop to purchase a city guidebook.

The doorman explained in broken English how to make subway connections to Stortorget Square, my first stop. I wanted to visit the restored Oslo Cathedral, completed in 1699.

Stortorget Square was bustling with bundled-up Norwegians sauntering about a huge flower market. The flowers, raised no doubt in hothouses or imported from Holland, filled bins at multitudes of stalls, adding a spring lilt to the bright, sunny day.

I suddenly felt homesick. The tulips jutting majestically from tin buckets reminded me of the Skagit Valley tulip fields back home in Washington. This brought on thoughts of Rene. I had taken my daughter one Sunday to see the tulip fields when she was five. "It looks like sunlight, Daddy. All yellow and gold. Look, some of them are just waking up."

I felt my eyes water at the memory. What was I doing here, a million miles from her? My emotions were getting away from me. I longed to hug her little body in my arms and kiss her. The letters to her were not nearly enough. I had called my parents once from Stockholm. The conversation was so stilted that I vowed not to call again. They didn't understand what I was doing over here. Even tried to talk me into coming back home. My sadness reflected consternation over why I didn't just leave.

I sat on a park bench in the cold for more than an hour, taking time to smell the daffodils and allowing my thoughts to linger on home for the first time since I started the tour.

Imagine! I was sitting in one of the world's most beautiful cities looking west at the snowy mountains west of Oslo, yet smelling flowers from home.

A huge ski jump on the lower slopes of the mountain in front caught my eye. The tour book called it Holmenkollen, home of the Holmenkollen Ski Festival held in March each year.

Finally, drawn by a powerful awareness, I headed across the street to the Oslo Cathedral.

The magnificent three-story-high doors, covered with bronze reliefs of ancient Norwegian religious leaders, welcomed me into the warmth inside. I wasn't prepared for the amazing four-story stained-glass windows of geometric patterns, figures, and even landscapes. The afternoon sun, beaming through sprayed rainbow-colored hues onto oak pews, added even more grandeur to this 300-year-old cathedral. I shuddered, feeling God's presence. I don't ever remember being affected so by divine power.

I lit a candle, then knelt and prayed at the altar, for Rene, my parents, myself. Despite the cathedral's coolness, guilt in the form of perspiration rolled down my face. I will never forget the experience of that moment. I felt God was touching my shoulder, letting me know he was still there watching and would protect me from dangerous curves in the Chippendale road ahead.

After a few more stops on the subway line, I arrived at Vigeland Sculpture Park. The entire landscaped area is dedicated to the imposing life's work of the remarkable sculptor Gustav Vigeland. His 192 sculpture groups in bronze, granite, and wrought iron depict the various stages of the human cycle from birth to death. The final display, completed in 1943, a year after Vigeland's death, is a powerful, moving piece — a monolith illustrating the struggle for life. The struggle for life . . . the struggle for life. The words embedded themselves in my mind.

I took two rolls of photos that day. The pictures still remind me of that isolated moment of both depression and euphoria that sunny day in Oslo, all alone and feeling lonely.

The next evening, Tuesday, it was business as usual. The show must go on. Thank God, the audience that first night at the Bryggeteatret Theater in Oslo was more subdued than those in Stockholm, if it's possible to rank levels of female screaming subtlety.

However, the audience did liven up during Gary's jungle scene, called, appropriately, "Cream." The number started with Gary lowering himself down a center stage rope, wearing a Tarzan-like thong, which the Breen Office wouldn't have allowed Johnny Weissmuller to wear in a million years, to the beat of music drowned out by drums. Once on stage, all alone, Gary half-pranced, half-stalked forward, feeling himself all over with splayed fingers to the accompaniment of pyro blasts on each side of the stage. Smiling his best come-hither look at the cheering audience, he dropped to all fours and slithered across the stage, crocodile-like, toward a wooden bowl of fruit front and center and pulled out an oversized banana.

With a wink at the ladies, Gary dropped to the stage floor and rolled onto his back, pulling up one knee. He positioned the banana upright at his crotch and started humping his rear upward while sliding both hands up and down the banana to the beat of the music. After a few more manipulations on the yellow fellow, it began spouting lotion out one end all over his naked chest, simulating a major tube tumult turnout.

He smiled at the audience, then stood, gyrating his body while rubbing the lotion sensually all over his chest.

The crowd went wild.

Gary shrugged, then, flaunting his hips, moved to a shower at back center stage and turned on the nozzle. The water worked this time. He leisurely washed his body, paying special attention to important parts. After a sudden Hercules-like pose flexing his muscles and a smile at the audience, the stage went black.

We never knew exactly what scene in the show would turn on the women the most, but this one was as good a stimulant as any.

The next morning, twelve of us bribed our bus

driver into taking us skiing at Hamar, a small town fifty miles north beside Mjosa, Norway's largest lake. This scenic spot was to be the site of the 1994 Winter Olympics. The mountains, fjords, and snow-covered mountains reminded me of the Cascades back home. We had scrambled for skiing gear, bought gloves and mittens, then of course rented skis and poles. We looked like the Mod Squad on a bad day, since no one had brought proper ski togs. We spent the day skiing Mt. Lille Hamar. I couldn't believe how inexpensive the lifts were, $20 U.S. for all day.

What a spectacular feeling schussing down the 7,000-foot mountain, looking at Mjosa Lake mostly thawed by the springtime sun. I was told the lake was where the famous Olympian and movie star Sonja Henie had learned to skate.

Mid-afternoon, Ernie, on his fourth run, just ahead and below me, barely missed a mogul, then hit a second one head-on, sending him sprawling on his back thirty feet into a snowdrift. His skis clung to his boots by the safety straps, preventing further problems of runaways that might have injured someone farther down the slope. I was the first to parallel stop near him.

"You okay?" I shouted.

Ernie wiped snow from his goggles. "I don't think so. Must have twisted my right knee. Hurts like a son of a bitch."

I pulled off my skis and sidestepped over. I knelt

beside him and felt around his kneecap. "Don't feel any breaks. Probably just pulled a muscle or something. Can you stand?"

I pulled him erect. He leaned on my shoulder.

Ernie said, "I've only been skiing a few times. Shouldn't have tried the intermediate slope. Too embarrassed to try the beginner." That was unusual to say the least, Ernie's admitting to being less than an expert on anything. "Don't tell anyone, okay?"

"Okay." I unclipped his ski safety straps.

"Try putting a little weight on your right foot."

He leaned on me more. "Ouch. I don't think so. Can't ski for sure."

I nodded. "Could have been a lot worse. Looks like you're through for the day. Stay up here while I find the ski patrol. They'll bring you down in a sled."

"You've got to be kidding. A fuckin' sled? Everybody on the mountain will know about it. Can't you just help me down?"

"No way, Ernie. It's too steep here. We'll both have an accident. I'll help you over to the trunk of that huge fir. You'll be out of the way of other skiers, and it'll be easy for them to find you."

I helped him off the trail through fresh snowdrifts.

Ernie said, "I'll be okay now, Troy. And . . . and, thanks for saving my ass."

That was the first time I ever heard Ernie thank anyone for anything. He was a hard-nosed, private person, concerned only about himself.

It took the best part of an hour to get the ski patrol up Lille Hamar and Ernie down to the ski operations lodge. I waited while the nurse on duty examined Ernie's leg. My diagnosis was right; he'd only pulled a leg muscle. He wouldn't be able to perform in the show that night for sure. As it turned out, he was out for three nights total.

Mark Pakin was really pissed at our skiing escapade, especially when he found out about Ernie. After all, Chippendales, Inc., had an investment in us that had to be protected. What if several had been injured? He'd have had to close the show.

That night at the Oslo after-hours nightclub selected for the evening, a hotel desk clerk groupie all the way from Stockholm showed up looking for me (third city she'd been to on the tour), acting as if we were sort of dating. It wasn't true, of course. This kind of thing happened more than once when girls followed me or some of the other guys from city to city.

I gave her the brush. Wanted something new tonight. While trying to avoid the groupie, I saw this great-looking woman, a petite, blue-eyed blonde, with high cheekbones and a smile I still dream about. From the way she was staring at me, I knew that friendship wasn't on her dance card. Katrina and I waltzed in broken English. The sexual energy was enough to singe a nun's twat in Alaska.

However, Tord, a Norwegian guy I had met skiing

that day in Hamar, had invited me to his flat for hash after the show, and I don't mean goulash! Hashish won out over sex, temporarily at least. I met Tord at his flat a few blocks from the nightclub, and we smoked for about an hour. Strong stuff. I was higher than a cathedral tower in minutes. We talked about skiing and the local girls. It was the first time I'd had a conversation in Europe with a man who was not a member of our company.

When I returned to the club, Katrina was still near the dance floor, waiting for me. I was still floating. The ten-degree temperature outside didn't faze me.

All I could think of was bouncing on a beautiful babe in a bed. It was a good hour's drive to our hotel. Couldn't wait that long. Besides, I hadn't made arrangements with Brent for use of our room.

I could tell Katrina was anxious when she started rubbing my dick through my jeans as if it needed thawing. She was right. The rubbing warmed it right up.

She whispered sweet-somethings in my ear and led me outside, then pointed up the hill. We struggled through the snow, intent on sex somewhere, anywhere. We'd stop every few yards to feel each other up and kiss, until my temperature was soaring. At the top of the hill, I pulled her into a small cemetery next to the church. Without preliminary, she unzipped me and started fondling. I reached under her skirt. No panties.

"We shouldn't be doing it out here. This is a cemetery, for Christ's sake." I emitted a half-assed moan.

"Don't you have someplace we can go?"

Her reply was a lip lock on my mouth that even Houdini wouldn't have been able to release.

She moaned as I fingered her, then pulled me down on top of her in the snow. I was too drunk and stoned to resist, even though we were only a few feet off one of Oslo's main downtown streets. We were soon fucking away, oblivious to anyone or anything.

About halfway to orgasm city, I looked up to find five grinning hippie types, rough-looking, bug-eyed, and cheering us on. Though the scene was on the wild side, it didn't faze me. I had to bury my own tombstone in the hole. The sexual spectators shouted something repeatedly in Norwegian. It sounded encouraging, though I was usually opposed to a peanut gallery.

I rose to the task, laughing and moaning. Katrina must have been freezing her backside off in the snow; however, her only complaint was "Close," then a bunch of Norwegian words.

We came simultaneously, shouting our pleasure into the dark loud enough to have awakened the dead buried about us. Grave concern was not on my "A" list. For all I knew, we were fornicating on one.

As I pulled her up and helped her brush off the snow, the male teenage voyeurs split. In my vulnerable condition, it was a wonder these peep-show pals hadn't tried to rob me or at the very least tried to fuck Katrina whether or not she agreed.

It could have been an ugly gang-rape scene.

We made our way, giggling, back down to the club. She agreed to meet me the next day at the hotel.

It turned out that Katrina was married to a Norwegian who owned a pizza parlor in the city. For the rest of my stay in Oslo, Katrina would deliver a pizza every afternoon to my hotel room at precisely two o'clock, and we would screw like crazy for an hour. A fuck a day keeps the doctor away, especially if it comes with a free pizza.

11

A week later, following pizza-for-two afternoons in Oslo, the troupe bused to Stavanger, Norway.

The trip west afforded the most dramatic scenery of any place I've ever been. I was seeing rugged nature at its most inspiring, enhanced by a glorious sunny day. The snow-enriched Folgefonne Mountains, rising sheer to great heights, rumbled north like pioneers in search of Iceland. The valleys were stark in relief, creeping toward glaciers so blue in the sunlight that they made my eyes water. Finally, glimpses of the sea peeked through drifting clouds. All around us, the glittering white stuff, sometimes at least fifteen feet deep, lay untouched and desolate, awaiting a spring thaw that would never arrive.

We headed down from a mountain pass to laborious sea arms probing far into western plateaus. "Breathtaking" is an adjective far too tame for this glorious mountain wilderness. I would someday have to return with Rene to this magnificent country the Vikings called Norway. Stavanger, at the southwestern tip, is the main North Sea oil base for the country. It acts and looks like an industrial town poised on the threshold of that labyrinth of Ryfylke fjords we'd crossed. It was a city of 80,000 or so Norwegians, particularly quiet Norwegians — so quiet that mention of the after-hours nightclub haunt of the Chips was deleted from Ernie's stage announcement during our only performance there.

Though Ernie was still in pain from his skiing accident, he was able to perform that evening. Ernie had visions of becoming a recording star. He was better at composing than singing. He'd written a musical dance number used in the show, "Apocalypse Now," a Vietnam War-type number with lots of pyro — guns shooting, grenades exploding, cannons blasting. Two other Chips wearing Army camouflage fatigues with ammo strung across their chests joined him on stage. The three performed a synchronized rifle routine. They were always practicing it backstage, sort of a therapy thing. At the end of the number, Ernie, alone center stage, pulled his fatigues off in one motion, leaving him sweating in thong and boots before a blackout.

It was a popular number.

Following the show that night, he invited me up to his room for pot and whatever and to thank me for my life-saving efforts on Lille Hamar.

When I arrived around midnight, he was alone, sitting cross-legged on his bed in his bikini underwear, stage makeup still on, strumming his electric guitar. I listened to his unfocused sad lament, then joined in. It was obvious that he was down. He'd been down ever since Hamar, and it didn't seem to have anything to do with his skiing accident.

It was also obvious he was high as Lille Hamar on something snowy. Coke — and I don't mean the diet kind. The residue of powder lay on the glass top of the nightstand like scattered flour. He'd obviously done a few lines.

We stopped singing, lit up a joint, and drifted with it.

Ernie's words were coke-thick. "Where is my . . . fuckin' life leading . . . Troy?"

I looked at him and shook my head. "Hell, I don't know. I ask myself that all the time."

Ernie continued, seemingly unaware I'd said anything. "I started this crap because I wanted to be somebody . . . ya know? Had to get out of Bakersfield. Had to get away from . . . Dad. You know, my mother was smart. She wised up and split when I was ten. Didn't take me or Timmy. Abandoned . . . that's what we were by a mom who didn't give a shit about us."

Ernie continued in a spaced-out manner. "He used to beat the hell out of me with a belt . . . for nothing, man. Fuckin' nothing. Maybe being the oldest. Never beat Timmy. Just me. Never praised me or anything.

Never cared what the hell I did. Never attended any of my track events. Never hugged me . . . made me feel wanted. Didn't even like me, the son of a bitch. He'd just pull out the old belt and start whacking for no reason. Well . . . maybe all the bourbon he drank had a part in it."

Ernie was wigging out.

He put a listless arm around my shoulder. "Never can go back."

"Why not?"

"Beat the shit outta the old man when I left, you know." He laughed hysterically.

"Knocked out his fuckin' teeth. Glad I did. He deserved more . . . the son of a bitch. Left poor Timmy to fight him alone. Never should have done that. Poor . . . Timmy."

He was pulling me down with his confession. "Tough, man. Really tough." I was beginning to understand why he was moody a lot. Pain and guilt. A reclusive formula if there ever was one.

I took another toke on the joint. "Where'd you go?"

He looked at me as though I was from outer space. "Go? Where the hell was it? Oh yeah. L-fuckin'-A. I had a little money saved. Eighteen and thought I had the world by the tail. Some tail! Didn't get any till I got a towel job in a gym." He laughed again.

I nodded.

"Beginning of my fuckin' show business career. Ain't that the shits? A fuckin' gym in Hollywood.

Started workin' out, buildin' these muscles." He flexed lazily. "Everybody thought I was a good-lookin' dude. Especially the wife of the gym owner. She was a sweet young bitch."

I nodded. "In heat all the time, right?"

He ignored my comment. "She got me interested in being a Chip. Next thing I knew . . . I was a waiter at the L.A. nightclub. Tough bitch of a job to get, too. Imagine, everybody fighting to be a . . . waiter, for Christ's sake."

He smiled dreamily. "Sweet job really. Those ladies loved me to pieces. Was makin' big bucks at nineteen too, all those women feelin' me up for tips. Made a Chipper stripper a year after that."

"No shit! Just like that?" I said.

He looked up at me for the first time. "Just like that."

He lay his head back against the headboard. "No . . . not exactly . . . like that. It took a little more fuckin' . . . even a rich sponsor chick."

Ernie choked and leaned forward. "Miss Rich Bitch, right? She paid for my membership in a real professional workout club. Paid for my own personal trainer. Bought me clothes and shit. Moved in with her. Hell, I'm swacked. Don't even know why the hell I'm tellin' you all this crap."

He knew, all right! He was obviously revealing more about his rise to stardom than he'd intended.

"Any-fuckin'-way, she knew Bannerjee and . . . and

129

got me in for an interview at Chippendales. . . ."

Mascara tears were running down Ernie's cheeks. I decided a piss break was in order.

"Hold the thought. Be back in a second, Ernie."

When I returned from the bathroom, I smelled smoke. Ernie had his cigarette lighter in his hand, waving it back and forth hypnotically, eyes focused on the flame.

"Ernie! What the hell are you doing?"

He wasn't lighting another joint; he was lighting the damn mattress! Tears were streaming down his cheeks. "Burn, Dad, you bastard!"

He smiled stupidly and lit the mattress ticking in another place. He was weirding out.

I grabbed the lighter and shut off the flame. Smoke filled the room. In seconds, the bedding was on fire. I pulled the sheets and blankets off the bed, rushed them into the bathtub, and started the shower. When I came back, Ernie was sitting on a side chair, head reeling, staring at the mattress, laughing crazily. I shook him until he realized what was going on.

It was too late to put out the smoldering mattress. No real flames yet.

"Window," I shouted.

We pulled the window up and squeezed the double mattress through. A strong sucking breeze worked in our favor. The mattress fell ten stories into a snow-shrouded courtyard to smolder another couple of hours. It's a wonder neither of us got burned.

We sat on the floor, lit another joint, and laughed until all the smelly residue was gone. If the old hotel room had been equipped with a smoke detector, we'd have been in shit city with management, both hotel and our own.

That was the end of Ernie's coke confession. He passed out, dried rivulets of mascara streaking his cheeks.

The next day, we said nothing about the incident or his confession. He never spoke that way to me again.

During the tour, the guys were responsible for thousands of dollars worth of damage to hotel rooms. None of them would ever own up to being the guilty party. Mark Pakin was always having to fork over damage money for destruction left in our wake. Sometimes the guys, stoned or drunk, would even piss on the hallway rugs, thinking it was all a great big joke.

I never did any of those things, but I watched a hell of a lot of crap going on and of course never ratted on anybody. Ratting, guaranteed to get your name embedded on the Chip shitlist of fame, was the cardinal sin. Never did understand what connection a stupid bird had with wrongdoing.

12

Our last show in Norway in the city of Kristiansand was uneventful. The audience of a thousand or so seemed more appreciative of our efforts and, at the same time, small-town subdued.

We spent most of April Fool's Day on ocean-going ferries heading east from Kristiansand, then north across the Skagerrak back to Oslo, where we switched to another ferry to head south again across the Kattegat back to our original home base, Copenhagen.

Scandinavia has perhaps the most extensive and efficient network of drive-on ferries in the world. The ships are spacious and comfortably appointed.

With my usual aplomb, I sought out and talked to a Scandinavian sitting in the lounge during this trip. He was a college student in his twenties from Copenhagen, returning from visiting friends in Oslo during his spring holiday. He spoke heavily-accented English.

When I asked about language barriers in Scandinavia, he told me that Danes, Norwegians, and Swedes could understand each other with relative ease. In Norway, the situation was slightly complicated by the fact that until 1905, when it seceded from Sweden, the official language was Danish. English was widely taught and spoken throughout Scandinavia, though less generally in Finland, especially among the older generations.

On the whole, there had been few areas of Scandinavia thus far where language barriers were a problem. Now I understood why.

It was good to be back in Copenhagen. Because most people here were fluent at English, I felt more at home than any other place on tour. Maybe it had something to do with Eileen, my medical student with the insatiable sexual appetite.

We arrived in Copenhagen about four p.m. Because we were not booked for a show that night, we were free to do what we wanted; however, the stagehands would be working, setting up for the performances starting the next evening.

One of the benefits of being a cast member in the production was never having to get my hands dirty with props and backdrops. I'm ashamed to say that, like the other cast members, I ignored the drones, acting like a queen bee when surrounded by the underling stagehands. If I had the tour to do over again, I would have been more appreciative of the hard work and long hours these drones spent on the anthill.

A stage production company is actually a functional accumulation of prejudiced humans. Strata of class abounds: hierarchy of show management looking down on lead performers, lead performers frowning on chorus dancers, chorus dancers steps above stagehands who tower over wardrobe people. All show business men and women thrive when with their peers. Their insecurities peek through, however, when their ideas of respect, privacy, and fear of the unknown are invaded by those of a higher strata. Bigotry, I discovered, plays the lead role in theater status and apparently always has.

At the crest of the insecurity pole, the star of the show stands alone, derisive of all beneath. He treats everyone with equal disdain — management, leads, chorus line, and stage help.

At least, Russell did. He was 6'5" and overly proud of being the tallest Chip. The star of our show had bared his butt on the glossy pages of Chippendale calendars for the past three years. He thought of himself as a Greek god in search of the Parthenon. He didn't drink, smoke pot, party, or hang out with the rest of us. He thought of his body as the Acropolis, each stone carefully stacked to a Adonis-like face.

Russell was a wanton exhibitionist. He enjoyed sauntering around backstage preening his magnificent naked body, as if to say, "You jerks don't know what muscles are all about."

Naturally, he didn't do steroids. He kept to himself, did his own thing.

His manner disqualified him from starring in a popularity contest. Being personable wasn't required for the job. He took full advantage of his advantage.

Weird guy!

Just for spite, I secretly hoped Russell would humiliate himself, you know, fall flat on his face somewhere during the tour so everyone could give him the horse laugh — lasso his arrogant attitude and hobble it, so to speak.

He never did anything to me personally; it was just that he was always so perfect. Mister goody-two-boots.

By seven o'clock that first evening back in Copenhagen, I still hadn't been able to reach Eileen by phone. I'd actually missed her. I'm not sure it was really her, the fantastic carefree sex she thrived on, or the sexual energy she pulled out of me.

Apparently, I wasn't to see her tonight.

By ten o'clock, I was sick of Danish television and ready for some action. I called first Cody's room, then Larry's, then Darrell's. None of them answered. Apparently, they'd flown the coop and hadn't invited this chicken along.

I tried Ernie's room. Bingo! After a few minutes of conversation, he convinced me we should try Club Copa, a strip joint on Vester Voldgade within walking distance of our hotel, just east of Tivoli Gardens. Though I had become wary of Ernie's suggestions regarding nighttime activity, we seemed to have developed some sort of bond that mattress-burning night.

By eleven-thirty, we'd smoked a couple of joints and headed for the hotel elevator. The next strip show at Club Copa started at the bewitching hour. It was as cold outside as a ride on a ski lift, well below freezing on the snow-cleared streets, typical weather for Denmark the first week of April.

At Club Copa, we tried unsuccessfully to sidestep the cover charge, based on our celebrity status as Chippendale dancers. Two strong does not a free entrance make.

We were ushered to a table jammed into a sea of other pizza-sized cocktail tables near the runway. It would be interesting to see how Danish women bared the bod. I couldn't help but compare the take-it-off styles with our guys' renditions. The bodies were good, breasts implanted to the max. The stripping was about as sophisticated as a banana peel, performed with the gusto of Patrick Swayze in drag. This was historic bump and grind. Nothing was left to the imagination for more than five minutes, or the crowd of drunk Danes got down and dirty. "Take it off . . . take it off" was honored to the max.

Twirl the twat in time to the tune took on a new tone. We were getting a bit drunk ourselves on vodka on the rocks. Ernie got into the spirit of the movement when one of the more gregarious performers slithered over to our table twirling her nipple tassels in front of his face. Was this a bust or what?

Jail time was not in question. *Playboy* centerfold beauties would have defected to *Hustler* with such tits.

Ernie tucked a twenty-krone note in her G-string, then kissed her bellybutton, adding a little tongue action. He always was a sucker for bellybuttons.

The next thing I knew, he'd invited Erika and her showgirl friend Jackie up to his hotel room for coke and cookies, without the cookies.

On the way back to the hotel, I said, "I'm pretty bushed. Think you can handle both of them?" I was leery this would turn into another orgy scene like with Christina in Stockholm. Even though Ernie's room had two queen-sized beds, I wasn't sure about these two queens. Might be a disease lurking somewhere between their legs.

"You kidding? The more the merrier. You not up to it, man?" Ernie teased.

"No, it's not that, it's just—"

"Too late to lose your virginity. Come on. You can have the one with the balloon tits."

Against my better judgment, Ernie twisted my arm. Or was it another part of my anatomy?

Besides, he'd given them his hotel key, the only way they could get into the hotel. Not a good idea in any country. What if they brought a couple of muscle guys to work us over and rob us? Or did it themselves? Stranger things had happened.

Ernie assured me, "These are legitimate working

girls. Both are billed on the Club Copa marquee out front. We know where to find them, right?"

"Yeah, and they know where to find us."

By three in the morning, soft knocks informed us our coke dates had arrived. A key in the door announced Erika and Jackie.

By 3:10, the girls and Ernie were sniffing coke and on a laughing high. I contented myself with a joint. I wasn't into harder drugs; hopefully, I would never be.

Before Jackie could say Robinson, the thirtyish stripper had her top off and was fondling Erika's nipples. Wait a minute! Something was rotten in Denmark. The girls were only interested in one another!

The women stripped off their stretch pants and G-strings fresh from their work-a-night runway and started fingering each other in wet orifices while tonguing their way to oblivion. That's a small town north of Copenhagen!

I didn't quite know how to react. Didn't know how to start anything. Wasn't anything to start actually. The showboat had already left the dock, and Captain Andy wasn't on board.

Ernie had picked up a couple of lesbians, into coke and each other, in that order. The girls were quickly on Ernie's bed, tongues running 69 miles an hour inside twin tunnels.

This was a new experience. Sex for two, all right. But two of the same gender. We were about as needed as clothes in a nudist colony.

Boy, the girls were getting into it. So was I — the erotic scene, I mean. The temperature rose south of my belt buckle.

I couldn't help myself. I was enjoying the show, too much. I yanked my zipper down, hauled out, and headed for the last roundup. The more the girls writhed, the more I pumped.

I think we reached euphoria at the same time. I'm not sure, but there was a lot of moaning going on, mine *and* theirs.

Neither Ernie or I got it on with the girls. After they'd finished each other, they washed up in the bathroom, thanked us for the refreshments, gave us pecks on the cheeks, and disappeared down the hall holding hands.

So much for lecherous lesbians!

Mid-morning the next day, after our Some Enchanted Evening, I finally connected with my Copenhagen cutie, Eileen. I invited her to lunch. She suggested a quaint smorgasbord restaurant in Old Town. We took an electric train across the city. Later, we did more of the sightseeing routine. I was appreciative of Eileen's desire to share her culture with me.

First stop, Vesterbrostorv and the Copenhagen City Museum. Fascinating Danish history in artifacts and paintings. Later, we consumed a people-oriented world history lesson by touring the famous Tussaud's Wax Museum located on the corner of Town Hall Square, one of the principal hubs of the city. Afterward, we stood in the square admiring the Jens Olsen World Clock and its Swiss, cuckoo-like figures prancing in and out of door openings. The clock is said to go through its routine every time a virgin passes by. Must be a lot of virgins in Copenhagen.

North of Stroget lies the neoclassical cathedral, the main building of the university Eileen attended. She proudly showed me the synagogue and the ten-story Round Tower built in 1642 by Christian IV. Its wide spiral ramp led us up to the Observatory and Astronomical Collection.

By four, we had enough touring. By 4:30, we were snuggled naked in her bed, sinking into a soft mattress, revisiting other territories of little or no historical significance.

Eileen invited me to stay in her spacious town flat during the rest of our Copenhagen engagement. Her wealthy father owned the building.

The extra bedroom was intended for female school friends or an occasional visit by strict father and mother. I don't think they had in mind an American boynik sleeping over. It was okay, though; I didn't occupy the spare bedroom.

By six that evening, I was at the theater, having dinner before dressing for the show. We were fortunate, or unfortunate depending on your point of view, to have Bill, our own company chef, traveling with us.

Bill, 56 and almost as tall as a Chip, was from London, espousing subtle English humor at will. He was a partially bald British version of Groucho Marx, complete with thick mustache and glasses. He was a well-respected, assertive chef who had toured with Genesis and Phil Collins prior to joining us. I wished I was making his kind of bread.

For some reason, Bill and I clashed. Maybe it was due to not understanding his sense of humor. Or was it because I was gluttonous at dinnertime? Low-fat, low-carbohydrate meals don't exactly fill up the tank of a six-foot-one frame.

Most of the guys resented Bill telling them they should eat healthfully all the time, even though he joked about it. Only Russell spoke Bill's language. The rest of us would sneak off for a Big Mac and fries at every opportunity. At least Ronald McDonald reigned in all the big cities.

Bill cooked dinner for us every day of a show, two hours before the performance. Mostly in the theater. We would gather at six and eat together. He insisted on preparing real healthful stuff. Chicken, fish, rice, vegetables. Low-calorie, low-fat, low-carbohydrate.

April 5 was Darrell's birthday. Our transplanted Chippendale from Houston, Texas, was to be 24, no longer a Chip babe in the woods after three tours of duty on the show's front line.

Eileen and I decided to give Darrell a good old-fashioned Texas barbecue. What's a barbecue? Eileen had no idea.

I clued her in. Grilled hamburgers with all the trimmings, potato salad, and baked beans. And lots of sissy garlic bread. Right? Not too hard to procure, even in Copenhagen.

Eileen and I had fun planning and gathering the fixin's, y'all.

Everybody in the Chippendale show cast was invited. Even Brent and his gay caballeros. Are you kidding? A hamburger away from dietetic dinners? They would have sold their thongs for such food fare.

Eileen invited a few of her school girlfriends to help out. Couldn't have all that meat and no potatoes!

Since we did not have a night off during the rest of our Copenhagen stay, Eileen and I planned the party on Darrell's actual birthday, April 5, early enough in the afternoon for everyone to be at the theater by 6:30.

The baked beans, Wenatchee-style, were the hit of the party. I came up with my mom's recipe — plenty of onions, molasses, and brown sugar, and baked for a good two hours.

Darrell's gag gifts were mostly sexual oddities: oversized condoms, a cock ring, a Swedish porn video, and a week's supply of pot (two days' worth for Darrell). His chin dimple quivered over his good fortune.

We were good that afternoon, drinking only soft drinks and forgoing drugs. We had a show to do in a couple of hours.

The troupe pretty much adhered to the rules for shows. No alcoholic beverages or drugs four hours before. Everybody except Cody, that is. He had his own set of rules. Everyone else laughed and had a great time throughout the party without the stimulant of either. Amazing!

We were late getting to the theater for makeup and costumes.

The opening number music started. Ernie took over Mark's usual opening remarks that evening with his standard, "Ladies, fasten your seat belts. It's going to be a bumpy night [burp] tonight."

Too much Texas food induced his unplanned vocal salvo.

The dancers sidled on stage. I was standing in the wings, feeling full. Even burped a couple of times myself.

Somebody farted behind me. Heads turned. Fingers pointed. We laughed. Nothing new about an occasional fart. By the time the entire group was on stage, though, a chorus of farts and burps were stinking up the stage. Everyone was looking at one another, snickering, wanting to hold their noses, but couldn't. Those Texas baked beans, via Wenatchee, had found their way to the bottom of the bod.

In planning the menu, I hadn't considered the culmination of gastronomic response. Neither had anyone else. Fortunately, the audience didn't get the drift of our stage mirth. The sounds of occasional gastric emissions were drowned in a sea of loud music — thank God for fortuitous booming!

We had inadvertently introduced a disco version of the famous fireside scene in the film *Blazing Saddles*. Mel Brooks couldn't have directed the scene better.

13

The credo "Getting there is half the fun" is a truism I was to experience on the overnight Viking Cruise Ship from Copenhagen to Helsinki heading back into the frozen north.

The sky was gray and the Baltic Sea calm when we set sail from the Copenhagen docks at seven (too early for human beings) on a Sunday morning the second week of April. However, we could sleep the morning away in four-bunk cabins on the lowest deck. Brent and I were joined by Jim and Barry, also on their first Chip tour. The berths were no more than two feet apart in a Tiny Tim-sized room. We had to dress and undress by the numbers, one at a time.

The leads, naturally, had their own one-bed staterooms, a deck above. The buses and semis, filled with sets of which Chip fantasies are made, nestled in the auto hold beneath us.

Eileen and I had said goodbye the previous night, finishing off a whole fifth of vodka. I would be back in the city one more time before the tour ended. Staying with Eileen had added a new perspective to the tour for me. Even calmed me down a bit. I had slowed up on the pot and vodka until the previous night. A touch of domestic life was what I needed. Eileen was a wonderful girl. I had learned to like her a lot. If things were different. . . .

No use thinking such thoughts. They were not different.

The Viking was one of the largest passenger/car ferry cruise ships in the world — all chrome and Danish modern right out of an Ikea store. Multiple decks, exercise room and sauna, and a nightclub complete with floor show and orchestra awaited our exclusive use. Not so exclusive. Eight hundred or so passengers were on board to share the simple luxury. This was to be a 24-hour cruise across the Baltic Sea, arriving in Helsinki at ten a.m. the following day.

Around six that evening, having toured the ship pretty much, I decided to check out the exercise facilities and Swedish sauna advertised in the ship service brochure in our room. A good sauna sweat would eliminate some of my hangover from last night's goodbye vodka at Eileen's. I checked in at the circular dispensing desk in the men's locker room, showing my stateroom key, and was given a towel. As I stripped in front of a locker, with perhaps a dozen fellow sauna users, two young girls in jeans and Viking Line T-shirts waltzed in to clean up. The other men seemed unconcerned, even though most of us were nude, or almost.

The college-aged girls went about their business, collecting towels and mopping up the floor, even in the adjacent shower room, oblivious to the naked males strutting about. Nudity was not a big thing in Denmark or Sweden. This lack of modesty on the part of everyone present but me was ample proof.

I fell asleep on a top step in the spacious sauna built for thirty or so naked, sweating bodies. Hangover perspiration spilled out my pores in buckets. Thank God, I was awakened by a fellow sweat-ee before I completely melted.

Thus rejuvenated, I was ready for a hair of a dog.

I sauntered into the dinner/nightclub looking for the gang. It was only eight o'clock, really too early for any kind of show. But I was hungry and Bill, our staff chef, had the night off.

Russell, our show star, sat alone in one of the banquettes, drinking. Must be ginger ale straight up, his usual. He waved me over. Unusual! We hardly ever spoke. "Have . . . a seat." His words were slurred. A look at his eyes told me ginger ale was not his drink of choice tonight.

"Have a vodka. Good for what ails you."

"Looks like it." I slid in and ordered a vodka tonic from the cute waitress, blonde, naturally.

Russell competed sip for sip for the next couple of

drinks while I awaited sea scallops in white wine sauce and a Caesar salad. I never did quite get used to European style, having salad after the entrée.

Russell became sullen, glancing repeatedly at a table a few banquettes away, seemingly lost in thought.

"You all right, Russell?" I managed between sips of vodka.

He looked at me. "Thinking of Carol."

I nodded. "She your girlfriend back home?"

"Was my girlfriend." His words were slurred. "We were going to get married. Poor Carol. All alone. You know, her father started molesting her when she was ten. Imagine! Ten."

Russell told me all about his high school sweetheart in Portland, Oregon, where they grew up, and their plans to marry and get her away from home. I hadn't known he was from my neck of the woods.

"She had a love/hate relationship with him. Never told her mother about it. Never could. Just me."

"Terrible. How could she go on living there?"

"Couldn't. That was the idea. After we graduated high school, we were planning to run away to L.A. and get married down there."

"Did you?"

He was lost in the vodka again. "All alone. She used to tell me about waking up in the middle of the night terrified, crying, visions of her father pulling her panties down clouding her nightmare. I wanted to smash her dad's face in, but she wouldn't let me near him."

Russell's expression drooped. "Then she was . . . killed in a car accident with one . . . of her girlfriends. Drunken driver. I-205. They were coming to a graduation party at my house."

I dropped my fork. "I'm sorry, man." What else could I say?

He nodded. "See the girl over there? The tall brunette between the two . . . blondes."

"Nice."

"Looks just like Carol."

His words were quiet, stilted. "Just like Carol. Her twin. Don't know why the hell I'm telling you all this."

I nodded. "It's okay. Sometimes it helps to talk about things." I was suddenly Doctor Joy Brown.

"After Carol . . . died, I went off the deep end." His glazed eyes were unfocused.

Knowing Russell, the deep end was probably eating a couple of almond Hersheys. I felt my cheeks flush. That was a stupid, insensitive thought.

"After graduation, all I could think about was Carol . . . me and Carol. You know, the Burger King where we liked to eat, the prom, what we were going to do with our lives in L.A. We never even had sex. Saving it for the honeymoon. Imagine a 19-year-old virgin in this day and age!"

"But how could she have been if her father had—"

"I mean me . . . I was still a virgin."

"Oh."

"Anyway, I got drunk for the first time in my life

the day after Carol's funeral . . . went to a whorehouse and screwed all night. Opened Pandora's box." He laughed, then shook his head slowly, a man drowning in sorrow.

"After Carol, I decided to head down to L.A. anyway. Had a pretty developed body, thought it might be my ticket to Hollywood. All through high school I had worked out three times a week at a Nautilus. I was proud of my body. Didn't even play basketball, though Coach Baldwin kept after me to. You know . . . tall. Gotta play basketball. My parents even paid for dancing lessons 'cause I said they'd be good for stretching my body. They were. Didn't take steroids or eat junk food. Still don't."

I nodded.

"So . . . packed up . . . said goodbye to everyone I loved, everyone who loved me. Went to L.A . . . without Carol." He was leaning back now, hand gripping the vodka glass as if someone was going to steal it.

"Did I tell you what happened . . . to her?" He was a tear away from a breakdown.

I nodded, and not so tactfully changed the subject. "How did you become a Chippendale? You never told me."

He looked up, stony expression altering his chiseled cheeks, and leaned over the table. "Got . . . job at Universal Pictures. Can you believe it? Just an extra, 'course. Pretty good dancer. Toned body. Kept working on it. Got a small dancing spot in *A Chorus Line*

. . . local stage production. Spotted by talent scout for Universal. Then did a couple of non-speaking parts in films." He was having trouble with his sentences.

He downed the rest of his vodka. "Did a bit part in Bruce Willis's third *Die Hard* movie. Bannerjee saw me . . . looked me up, and voilá! A Chip. Three years ago. Still dancin'."

"I guess so. And star of the show. You're doing all right."

"All right?" He slammed his empty glass on the table top.

"All right? Stripping naked before a bunch of screaming women every night is all right? Basement of show business. Classy pornography. What can it lead to?"

I quipped, "Maybe a singing career for me. Hollywood . . . TV?"

I was shocked he was so down on his chosen profession.

"Get real, Troy. It's a job. A dirty, good-paying job. I discovered the hard way. The big guys don't want men who are kissing cousins to a porno flick." He shook his head. "And just think about it. How long can I do this stuff after thirty."

He was still seven years away. I was only two!

Russell pushed out of the booth. "Gotta take a leak."

While he was gone, I thought about his words of wisdom. He was a star, but by his own admission, star of what? I hadn't slowed down my hell-bent pace enough to analyze my situation from his perspective. All of us were in imminent danger of abs sagging, wrinkles appearing which no amount of makeup could disguise. What woman wanted to watch the geriatric set stripping? Becoming too old for the game fell into that of the aging athlete, dancer, and film star.

Was this why I was here, hanging my voice on a peg called discovery by a European movie mogul? Unless she was female, she wouldn't even see our show. Such dilemmas filled my mind with ghost-like images. I had drawn a DMZ line. The excitement and fun of the chase for sex and drugs on one side, my side-railed career on the other.

When Russell returned, he had the Carol-lookalike girl in tow. "Troy . . . meet Carol. No, that's not your—"

"Ingrid." She smiled. She, too, was a couple of sheets to the wind and there was no wind.

She was Dutch, brunette, at least five-feet-ten or so. Not beautiful, but dark-skinned and young. Her long eyelashes leaned a little to starboard, as though she'd chugged a couple of martinis before applying them. Gave her sort of naive Mata Hari look with her secrets for hire.

By the time she and I had become acquainted, struggling through broken English, and finished another drink, I was impressing the early crowd filling the nightclub for the ten-o'clock show with my vocal talent, singing karaoke. At least, Ingrid was impressed.

Russell continued to call her Carol, sinking lower and lower into the lounge until he laid his head on the table and passed out.

I shook him awake and suggested I take him to his stateroom. I was now having trouble maneuvering myself.

"Nope. I can make it. Take care of Carol, will ya?"

Take care of her, I did. Ten minutes after Russell's departure, Ingrid and I were downstairs in her stateroom doing the dirty deed. Like my stateroom, it had four bunk beds. Her two female roommates were asleep on the other bunk, so we tried to be quiet while ripping off our clothes. In my drunken state, I was more like a bull in the pen waiting for the picadors. Kept running into the cape, or was that the drape?

Ingrid and I were naked and fucking under the blanket of her bunk in less time than it took to play *The Minute Waltz*.

Her friends were pretending to sleep while I played beach blanket bingo under the covers. The first thing I knew, the two blonde girls had turned on the light. They were holding up our blanket, watching me punch the number in the circle.

What does a gentleman do in such a situation? He asks all players to join the game. Ingrid, who had lost the wayward eyelash somewhere in the bedding, said something long in Dutch. I didn't understand a word but got the drift because, in a flash, the girls' nightgowns lay in a heap on the cabin floor.

A squealing, feeling frenzy erupted before I could figure out how a foursome could possibly fool around at the same time, especially in such a narrow bed. I soon decided that orgies in a lower bunk should be added to the agenda for the Olympic Games. Such imaginative sport!

Must have been enough of me to go around. I know there were enough of them.

I awoke with daylight streaming through the cruise ship porthole, stabbing my hungover eyes. I was on a lower bunk (not the one on which I had started) with my back cramped against the wall, and Ingrid — I think it was Ingrid, yeah, she had black hair — curled naked and spoon-like against me. The other girls were in the opposite bunks, snoring. I didn't even remember falling asleep. I wasn't too sure what we did, but I remembered running out of condoms. It must have been fun.

I dressed and slipped out of the room without awakening anyone. I had only an hour to take a shower and get ready to exit the ship.

Never did tell Russell what he'd missed. Ingrid was great. At least, I think it was Ingrid.

I made it up on deck of the Viking in time to watch the ship dock at the mouth of the River Vantaa at Helsinki South Harbor. From my bloodshot eyes, the snow-covered city of half a million or so looked drab.

Of course, my view was tempered by the grandeur of Copenhagen, Stockholm, and Oslo — beauties all — and my sunglasses. Helsinki looked rather like a dull Russian cousin just off the train from Siberia.

This main section of Helsinki was a peninsula linked by bridges, causeways, and boat services to the widespread suburbs and satellite towns.

South Harbor, as the area is called, was bustling with a morning open-air market even though it was only ten a.m. Below, vendors were hawking fresh fish, flowers, fruits, and vegetables as well as handicrafts and household goods, to mostly locals. It was too early in the year for tourist-season patrons.

Overlooking the harbor was the red-brick Uspenski Orthodox Cathedral, the President's Palace, and Town Hall. I didn't know what the buildings were until I took a short tour the next day. None of the historic buildings particularly impressed me.

At the hotel (I forget the name), Cody made such a scene about the scuzzy lobby that we never made it to the rooms. The only thing keeping that dump from falling down was the termites holding hands. Everyone chimed in that we weren't staying.

Thank God, Mark Pakin was forced to find us better accommodations.

At five-thirty that evening, two hours after moving into the four-star Inter-Continental Hotel, our bus carried us down one of the main streets of Helsinki to our show home for three nights, the City Theater.

Up ahead, a crowd of people waved signs. Must be some sort of strike going on, maybe nurses against a hospital or construction workers picketing a building.

Our bus stopped right in the middle of the mostly male throng.

A hundred or so bundled-up Finns were thrusting signs skyward as if their will be done. Because none of us could read the local language, we were unaware that these were foes, not fans. They were not unhappy male nurses or construction workers, but angry husbands and fathers protesting our performance that evening.

When our bus door opened, we filed into an angry crowd pressing forward, shouting Finnish and pointing dagger fingers at us.

I noticed the drawing on one of the signs: a banana, with a no-smoking-type red slash across it. Somebody had heard about the orgasmic squeeze in our second act. At least our show's fame had crossed the Baltic Sea to Finland.

A number of Helsinki police quickly surrounded us. Eager male hands trying to grab us was a new experience. The chicken had not come home to roost, however; these turkeys were interested in tearing off a drumstick or two, not our feathers.

Once we were safely inside the City Theater, the manager apologized profusely to Mark Pakin and the rest of us. It seemed that a Bible belt group from Tampere, a small town east of Helsinki where we were to appear for one night later in the week, had traveled all the way here to get their kicks in early. When asked, the manager interpreted some of the signs. Loosely, they meant in English: "No smut. We don't want naked. Go home, American naughty boys. No sex shows for our children." We got the drift.

All the hype, duly covered by the Helsinki news media, was a godsend. The shows here had not been sold out. Now the second and third nights were. Such is the power of television and the mighty press.

It wasn't until we were back on the bus heading from Helsinki to Tampere later in the second week of April that I found out what Ernie had been doing during my masturbation madness marathon with those lesbian strippers in Copenhagen.

The guys on the bus were whiling away the time with nothing but boring Finnish landscape eking by, showing videotapes on the TV monitor. Suddenly, two women were on a bed, naked and tongue-locked in each other.

Ernie's hotel bed!

Shit! You got to be kidding! I didn't remember Ernie filming that evening. I hope he didn't — "Shit no!" someone shouted above the clamor. It took a second to realize it was me. I was suddenly right there in living color for all the world to see. Little ol' me. Only I wasn't so little. The old Wenatchee boy stood there proud of his worth hanging out of his jeans, stiff as a pot pipe. More.

My hand was playing *Dixie* on the flute, very un-flute-like.

The Chips went wild, cheering, whistling, and pointing.

My God! Nothing is sacred. I already said that, didn't I? Well, it isn't. If there had been a way to jump off the bus, I would have. I felt the color blasting my cheeks. How could Ernie do such a thing to me? I thought he was my friend. I glared back at him. He pointed at my dumbfounded expression and laughed even harder.

What else can you do when your anatomy is responding from right-handed enthusiasm? Rectify the ridiculous by treating the exposure as the practical joke it was meant to be, laughing at my own expense.

For at least a couple of weeks after that, I smoldered over the humiliation, the invasion of my privacy.

Finally, the "why not?" syndrome eased the embarrassment from my libido for the rest of the tour.

It took me until the bus trip back to Helsinki to get even with Ernie for his little exploitation of my feeling frenzy.

Mark Pakin missed our show that night in Tampere. He stayed in Helsinki to arrange our plane trip to Brussels. Fortunately, he missed the abuse and mistreatment out front of the theater by the Bible-belting boys bent on bad-mouthing us.

That evening, Ernie, in his capacity as master of

ceremonies, got angry backstage following his war number. He was very particular about the stage lighting and sound, especially during the scene he'd written. His number was screwed up that night with missed cues and pyro going off seconds late. In the wings, he yelled at James, one of the older stagehands, until I thought everyone in the audience would hear the commotion. James threatened to quit on the spot.

Ernie had so much power as a lead that he could get away with almost anything, including berating the hired help. Star power. Not an admirable affectation.

I knew Ernie's anger wasn't spent and had my trusty miniature hand recorder ready and waiting.

Not to my surprise, Ernie, standing alone on stage in his master of ceremonies role, started taking out his ire on the mike, cursing out the women in the audience in English using cute little phrases such as "You fuckin' bitches are dumber than shit; come up here and chew on my dick; you're nothing but sleazy sluts" and other words to that effect. I got it all on tape.

The Finnish ladies out front, who didn't speak a word of English, cheered, no doubt thinking he was saying something sexy, even complimenting them.

Ernie had done this bit in Norway one night, so I expected him to be up to his asshole in slander tonight. He had good cause — the botched-up scene he'd just danced through and the picketers protesting male comeliness out front.

The next morning during the bus trip back to

Helsinki, I turned the recorder on full volume. Ernie's tirade played to our bus-captive audience better than a new Michael Jackson CD.

Ernie really got pissed at me.

I was even.

Or so I thought.

As Cody later explained to me, my get-even joke could have backfired big-time if Mark Pakin had gotten wind of the tape. Ernie would have been fired. Possibly me, too.

14

Sunday morning, the third week of April, we boarded a plane in Helsinki en route to Brussels, Belgium. The sets and props had been relegated to a barge chugging across the Baltic Sea, which would take two days. This time lag gave us an equal amount of much-needed rest from back-to-back shows before hitting the stage again. We were to make Brussels our headquarters for the rest of the tour with side trips to Antwerp, Belgium; Dusseldorf, Germany; and Lille, France.

The plane was overbooked, apparently not an unusual phenomenon in Scandinavia. By the time I boarded late, ten minutes after the other Chips, I discovered my seat was already occupied. It had been double-booked. Lucky me! The only vacant seat on the plane was in first-class on the row just behind the galley and pilots' cabin. It was the first time I'd ever sat in first-class.

As I stretched out in the wide, comfortable seat, I eyed the attractive brunette woman sitting across the aisle. She was forty-looking, wearing an expensive brown pantsuit and enough gold jewelry to put Mr. T to shame. Interesting! Her smile seemed more than welcoming. I introduced myself. She nodded, then said something sounding like Finnish. We would not be able to communicate verbally; however, her constant smoldering looks were enough to sizzle my bacon.

Free champagne preceded a delicious filet and scalloped potatoes served on china. Imagine! Silver utensils, white linen placemats, and cloth napkins on an airplane. I could get used to this kind of travel.

The brunette and I continued flirting all through dinner, eye contact filled with suggestive nuances. Following the chocolate mousse and espresso, she unbuckled, stood, and stepped into the aisle, then headed into the toilet. She gave her ass an inviting wiggle, then winked at me while licking her full lips, and she didn't even know I was a Chippendale.

The positioning of my first-class seat gave me an unobstructed view of the interior of the toilet when a passenger opened or closed the door.

For some reason, after closing the toilet door, the lady failed to pull the "Occupied" lever. My mind works in predictable ways. Was this some sort of invitation to join the Mile-High Club? Hell, there wasn't enough room in one of those johns for me, let alone the two of us.

Before I could decide what to do, the pilot cabin door swung open and a medium-built pilot in a small-built uniform stepped out.

He stood just in front of me with his hand on the toilet door handle, smiling the captain's welcome to all up front.

No! my mind wanted to shout. I straightened. "There's someone—"

Too late! He opened the door and stepped right into panties and pants looped around the lady's ankles. The lady and the captain yelled simultaneously, loud enough to alert everyone in first-class that something was amiss, or was it a miss was something. I think I yelled, too!

The captain's foot was inextricably tangled in her clothing. He pulled his foot back immediately, yanking her clothes with it. This counterproductive move pulled her naked ass forward off the seat and onto the toilet deck, legs and wayward clothing now thrust into the first-class aisle. With the clothes still snuggled around his right foot, the captain backed into a stewardess in the galley behind him who was holding a tray of after-dinner drinks. The liquor flew everywhere, as did the captain and stewardess.

All I could do was laugh at the slapstick routine right out of *I Love Lucy* taking place directly in front of me. I didn't know whether to help untangle the unmentionables or help the half-naked lady back onto the toilet. So I did nothing. The stewardess saved the day, crawling from beneath the captain, ignoring the drink mess, and pulling Sitting Bull's foot free of black panties and brown pants. She asked the lady, "Are you all right?"

The lady said something in Finnish. The stewardess nodded, said something back in Finnish, and helped the mortified lady back onto the toilet seat.

The lady saw me laughing. Her face flushed darker. The stewardess closed the door, smiled at everyone as though this sort of thing happened every day, then turned back to the captain, who was trying to sponge syrupy liqueurs off his uniform.

This time the "Occupied" light came on.

So much for joining the Mile-High Club.

Our room at the Amigo Hotel in Brussels was very modern, complete with kitchenette. Because the weather outside was frightful, drenching rain, my roommate, Brent, suggested we stay in, broil steaks, and bake potatoes in the microwave. We'd been cool toward each other since the big stage fight in Arhus, Denmark.

Eating in sounded like a good idea. I volunteered to face the elements to get groceries.

After salad and dinner at the small dining table, we popped the cork on the second bottle of French burgundy. Brent and I were soon into life and spiritual growth — where we were coming from, where we were going. He put on his favorite cassette, the cast album from *Miss Saigon*. Beautiful duets and solos reverberated about the room. While we listened, Brent told me of his love for musical theater. I'd never truly listened to this kind of music before. I was aware of it, of course, but had never truly listened. Thanks to Brent, I learned to appreciate the art form that evening.

We were mellow on the wine. No drugs tonight. Just cigarettes. I couldn't get chewing tobacco in Europe, so had resorted to Joe Camels.

Brent coughed. "Why the hell are we smoking these cancer sticks?" He coughed again.

"How the hell do I know? Stupid, I guess."

He mashed the butt of his in the ashtray. "We ought to quit here and now."

"Think so?" I was agreeable.

"Just a minute." Brent found a glass candlestick fully loaded in the kitchen. He put it in the middle of the table and lit the candle. We clicked wine glasses. "Fuck the tobacco industry!"

"Fuck the tobacco industry!" I repeated.

We laughed. I was beginning to feel a bond with Brent, seeing him in a new light.

Somehow, the time seemed right to ask the big question: "When did you first think you were gay?" Maybe some inside knowledge might help me get over my Cantata of Homophobia.

He sort of half-smiled and nodded. "I wondered when you'd ask. Your type always does."

My type? I started to say something smart-assed,

but held my tongue. "You don't have to tell me if you don't want to."

Brent said, "No. I don't mind. Never told anyone straight. Thirteen. I was thirteen."

That young? I thought.

"A guy who lived next door in Santa Barbara had a couple of porno magazines he'd swiped from his brother. Straight ones. We started jerking off to them. You know, kid stuff. Pretty soon it became more than kid stuff."

I said, "Sounds familiar. I did the same thing."

He smiled, "You jerked off with a friend?"

"No," I said quickly. "I mean I swiped a *Playboy* from my brother's collection and jacked off. I was alone though."

Brent said, "Not quite the same. Anyway, I found myself staring at the big peckers, not girls' anatomy. Only the peckers. I was fourteen when I had sex with a man for the first time. I looked much older because of my height — already five-eleven. You should have seen my ears then. My body grew up to the promise of them.

"My first real sex with a male happened in a Santa Barbara park not far from my house. Guy must have been in his twenties. He was in jogging shorts and tank top, and stopped deliberately to rest on the bench I was sitting on alone. He rubbed a sweaty leg against mine. I didn't move. The next thing I knew, his hand was on my crotch feeling me up. He led me back into the bushes. I was scared out of my gourd, but followed him anyway. I wanted it as much as he did. He rubbed me all over. In nothing flat, he had my hard-on out and was playing overtures with his mouth. I never felt anything so wonderful."

Brent swallowed the last of the wine in his glass. Did I really want to hear all this? Shouldn't have asked the question in the first place.

"Anyway, I still didn't think of myself as gay. In the gym locker room at school, I was more than interested in all the naked male equipment, though. I'd get an embarrassing erection every day at shower time. Had to hide it with a towel.

"I never let myself do anything other than masturbate with my friend for the next few years. You know, playing with each other a little. No mouth action."

I poured us another glass of wine.

Brent continued. "All through high school, I worked out. Swam, surfboarded in the Pacific. Developed these pecs. I was hit on all the time by women as well as men. I stopped wearing a bikini to the beach. Switched to baggy swim trunks. I didn't know who I was, or that my sex life was all screwed up. I knew I didn't like to date. Even tried sex with one of my high school girlfriends once. It was a disaster. I couldn't get an erection for the life of me. She didn't understand why. I did."

Brent took a sip of wine and started in again. "It really wasn't until I was eighteen and graduated from

167

high school that I really started asking myself questions. I knew the answers, but didn't want to acknowledge them. I thought seriously about killing myself."

"No. Really?"

He nodded. "You don't know what it's like to have all these unanswered sexual questions about yourself rolling around in your brain, and not having anyone with whom to confide. You're ashamed of yourself, thinking it's not right, embarrassed that someone might find out. You're being sinful and all that garbage, even though it's really meant for you. The guilt! Man, the guilt eats you alive. My parents would have had conniption fits had they known what I was thinking and doing."

I nodded. It was sort of like what I was doing now on tour. My dad would have a stroke if he knew how I spent the nights following our tour shows.

Brent leaned back in the chair. "They didn't have the money to send me to college, so I joined the Air Force with my high school jack-off buddy, Ted. The Air Force would straighten me out for sure. I was convinced of it."

I chuckled. "Guess they didn't."

He nodded. "You're getting ahead of me. It wasn't until then that I started coming out of the closet.

"I was still confused by all these thoughts, thinking this was some kind of phase that I'd grow out of. The confusion remained. I was obsessed with the idea of having real sex with a male."

I said, "Everybody had questions about sexuality at that age."

"Did you?"

I thought a second, then shook my head. "Shit, I was married by the time I was nineteen. Didn't think about having sex with anyone but my wife. And it wasn't very good . . . a lack of chemistry between us."

Brent nodded. "What made me different from you? Something I was born with . . . different genes, I suppose. Being homosexual isn't something a guy just decides to become one day . . . joining some sort of gender sect on a whim. It's something all gays learn to understand and accept. It's karma. The way the ball bounces . . . karma. We don't want anyone to feel sorry for us, or think some psychologist is panting just around the corner to get hold of our psyche and turn the toggle switch to 'normal' again."

Brent was really screwing my head up now. Church had taught me that homos were abnormal. But Brent didn't act or talk abnormally. How could that be?

He straightened as though his revelations were somehow therapeutic. "In Air Force basic training, I started having even more problems with my head. Should I or shouldn't I let myself relax and participate in gay life? That's a dangerous, difficult question to ask yourself, especially while you're eighteen and in the service."

He looked up at me. "Some guys never get past the question. They kill themselves."

169

I felt stupid. I'd never given a second thought to the problems afflicting men wrestling with such ideas. Could what Brent was saying be true? I still had doubts. His must be an isolated case.

"Those big open shower rooms in basic training school were my undoing. I was back to hiding constant boners again, trying my best to shower alone, yet at the same time not wanting to."

All through this, Brent's voice was steady. I could detect no embarrassment in his demeanor as he presented his story in a straightforward, casual manner. I could never have confessed such a thing to another man, especially a straight one.

"I was stationed at Travis Air Force Base, near San Francisco, haven of gaydom," Brent continued. "I just had to get to Frisco and find out what gay life was all about.

"I went off the deep end."

He shook his head. "Boy did I ever. Went AWOL. Hitchhiked up 101. The guy who picked me up was a real queen. 'Effeminate' took on new meaning. I wasn't in his old Thunderbird five minutes before he was asking to feel my arm muscles. I said sure. I wanted him to. Maybe this would be the real initiation I was hoping for."

He chuckled, letting me know he was comfortable telling me all this.

"We were off the highway in a roadside park quicker than he could get my uniform zipper down. He played mouth organ like a pro. And I . . . I did him, too. First time ever."

Brent stared at the rain on the windowpane.

I blurted, "You don't have to—"

He looked back. "This helps, somehow, Troy. I'd forgotten those feelings of coming out. They were pretty brutal. I appreciate your listening, especially knowing how you feel about homosexuals."

It was my time to be embarrassed. I felt my face flush. "I guess I had that coming."

"It's all right. At least you're willing to look at the other side of the coin now."

I nodded.

"That weekend, I discovered Polk Street and Polk Street discovered me. My looks and muscled body had the guys crawling out of the woodwork. Fresh meat on Polk Street. I still only let guys do me. I was a top."

"A top?"

"That's the screwer, not the screwee. We would do everything in the park, in their pads, hotel rooms. Everywhere, really. The dam had broken and I wasn't sticking a finger in the dike even though the flood wasn't far behind.

"It only took a couple of days to be picked up by Gary, this GQ-dressed older guy who invited me to his townhouse for a week of fun and games. It was becoming a very long AWOL weekend — what's more, a quick education I hadn't learned in school. He was the first to, you know, screw me. I liked it. I knew for certain I was gay then. No doubt about it. I wasn't the devil incarnate; I was just horny for men."

Brent walked to the window, then turned back. "You don't want to hear all this shit, do you?"

I didn't say a word. Just looked at him. It was a time for quiet. A sort of spell came over the room. Understanding drifted around like Caspar the Ghost on holiday.

Brent walked back and stood behind the empty chair. "My mentor was forty-five with a tall, slender, beautiful body I craved.

"Gary talked me into going back to base and turning myself in, or I'd be ruined for life. He promised to help me if I needed him to. It was a tough decision. I'd found my hard in San Francisco." He laughed again.

I detected the hurt in his voice.

"Instead of a court-martial and stockade time, the Air Force felt it necessary to dishonorably discharge me from the service."

"No shit! Dishonorable discharge?"

"Yes. AWOL, absent without leave, during basic training. But the real problem was my stupidity, telling my company commander the reason I left the base. AWOL he could deal with. Homosexuality he couldn't, especially with idiots who confess to the crime of the century, accented with tears of shame."

I said, "They discharged you for being gay?"

"Yes. Don't tell . . . don't ask! Shattered that fuckin' rule in spades." He sighed.

"My parents were told the whole story by my commanding officer. My father shit a brick. Said I could never . . . ever come home again. He hadn't raised me to become a fag." Brent choked on the words and remained silent.

"Your own father said that? Damn!" I was speaking just above a whisper. So was he. I wanted to hug him, but he might misconstrue the gesture as some sort of affection. No, to be honest, he would have accepted it for what it was, a friend showing concern. It was me who couldn't bring myself to hug a queer.

I managed, "Thank you, Brent, for sharing this with me. It helps me understand a little. Never talked to a gay person before you . . . never like this. I had no idea what being gay was all about."

He was still quiet, staring at the wineglass, then looked up, tears welling in his eyes. He took a swipe with the back of his hand. "I've kept that story bottled inside so long. It's been eating me up for years. Never told anyone . . . about those things. You know, the details.

"I don't know how to say it, Troy, but talking to you like this helps me get through all my shit . . . loss of my family and all. You don't know how it feels, to have been hugging close to your parents all your life, feeling and knowing the love from them all the time, then having the affection door shut in your face . . . set adrift with a 'Don't come back home . . . ever.' "

His words were chilling. Hugging close! Don't come

back home . . . ever! "What about your mother? What did she have to say?"

"Nothing. That was even harder. Fuckin' nothing. She went along with Dad. That was the biggest blow. She said nothing."

I felt his sadness. "Did you ever try to go back? You know, face them in person?"

Brent looked up. "No. Never. Dad didn't allow for any conditions. The last time I called, Dad said I was no longer a son of his. I'm an only child, too. Didn't make any difference. Guess it still doesn't.

"Never . . . can go back. 'Never' is a long time."

His sigh was tortured. Then he started in again. "After my dismissal from the Air Force, I went back to Gary, my older friend in San Francisco. He had all the best exercise equipment. Built me up more. Got a job in a male strip joint in the Tenderloin. Gary didn't like that one tiny bit. He knew all about the Chippendales in L.A., said if I was going to strip, might as well get into legitimate show business where I could make some decent money. Ha! Legitimate show business. Isn't that a joke!

"Anyway, he helped me get an interview. I had the body and the height and already knew how to dance and strip. I was good, too."

I nodded. "You are good. Everybody knows it. The best dancer in the show by far. Sorry I never told you that."

He smiled. "Thanks, Troy. That means a lot. Anyway, I left Gary to join the Chips three years ago after only being with him a year. I write him sometimes. Isn't that something? He was responsible for my leaving him, helping me get into the Chippendales. Being kind, looking out for my welfare.

"I guess Gary knew I was never going to stay with him. He was older, I wasn't in love with him . . . then. I think I am now. Big mistake leaving him. Should jump ship and go back to Frisco."

I hesitated. "If that's the way you feel, why don't you?"

"Commitment to the production, I guess. Besides, all the sex games are great fun. Of all people, you know all about sex games."

I felt my cheeks flush.

He added, "A new guy in every city. Besides, Gary probably has a new boyfriend by now." He laughed, then shut the door to his former life.

"Here's to no smoking." He threw his pack of cigarettes into the trashcan.

I thought I had problems. Nothing like Brent's.

We finished the wine, then put on the cast album for *Phantom of the Opera*. We became good friends that evening, an actuality I wouldn't have thought possible.

15

The next morning in Brussels, spring was in the April air. The wind had died. The sun was doing its damnedest to warm the cobblestones. The previous night's rainstorm had washed away Ol' Man Winter's cobwebs.

Brent invited me on a tour of the city. Together? Just the two of us? I was worried for a moment that the other guys would see us palling around and think . . . to hell with what they thought.

I was flattered he asked me. Tolerance had hit me on the head and made a dent.

Brent, having been here on tour previously, was the perfect guide to the city. On our walk from the hotel, he explained that Brussels had visions of becoming the capital of Europe, since it was already the home of the European Commission.

Our first stop was the Grand' Place, just a few

blocks away from the Amigo Hotel. I stopped in my tracks, gaping in wonder as we walked into the huge square. It was as though the pearly gates had opened in front of me. The ornamental gables, medieval banners, and gilded facades of the buildings made me feel like I'd just stepped out of a *Back to the Future* time machine, sweeping me back through the centuries to the days of powerful guilds and barons.

Brent laughed at my expression. "Affected me the same way the first time I saw this. Amazing, isn't it?"

I could only nod.

"Those are Flemish Renaissance buildings dating from the late 1690s. This was the headquarters of great trading and mercantile guilds: tailors, butchers, brewers, bakers, cabinetmakers, and the like. It's the most beautiful square I've seen in Europe. Last year when we were here in May, the entire center of the square was filled with elaborate flag-type designs made up entirely of real flowers in bloom. Wonderful! And wait until you see this place at night. Awesome!"

We stopped at Le Roy d'Espagne to spend our francs on coffee and mouth-watering Belgian cakes.

Brent stated, "In another month, the sidewalk cafes will be open all around the square."

Black bicycles seemed at home in outside racks everywhere I looked. How was anyone able to distinguish their own?

Our next stop was at Bruparck Theme Park, a Belgian version of Disneyland.

We stared at the symbol of the city, the Atomium, a futuristic structure of nine huge spheres linked by tubular rods representing the atomic structure of iron.

Brent chimed in, "It was built for the 1958 World Exposition. Fabulous, isn't it?"

"Different" would be my assessment. Looked like something from outer space had landed in Brussels and had coveted the atmosphere.

"Too bad we can't see the park. Doesn't open until May. Mini Europe is worth coming back for. Look over there. You can see the top of the Leaning Tower of Pisa and the Arc de Triomphe."

I said, "That I'd like to see."

"There's more. Each of the twelve European Community countries are represented with famous buildings and structures done in a 1.25-inch scale."

We visited the Musée d'Art and saw paintings by Belgian old masters Brueghel and Rubens, then went to the Great Cathedral Saint Michel. The Catholic church's fantastic stained-glass windows reminded me of my moments of loneliness and reverence in Oslo Cathedral.

At my suggestion, Brent and I lit separate candles and spent a few minutes kneeling in prayer. How could one not do so in such a sanctified atmosphere? At the same time, I was discovering Brent's depth of soul. He was a genuine man, perhaps the only genuine man besides my mentor back home, James, that I'd ever known.

Our last stop was at the statue *Mannekin-Pis* on the corner of Rue du Chene.

Brent said, "There he is, pissing away like crazy." It was the famous statue of a little boy doing it with all the gleeful verve of any little boy who's ever taken part in a "Let's see who can piss the farthest" contest.

Our tour ended at the Amigo Hotel and dinner with the rest of the guys. Bill, our company chef, had arrived. Damn! We were on the low-calorie-count carousel again.

The grand tour of Brussels that day cemented my relationship with my gay roommate. I no longer worried about Brent hitting on me, or what the other guys thought about our friendship. He'd become a person to me, sincere and real.

On Friday night of that third week of April, we opened at Theater 140, so named because of its location, 140 Avenue Plasky. It was one of the better theaters housing our show on the tour. Even the dressing rooms were clean and well-lit.

We were rejuvenated after three days off, and back in a big city again. The house was sold out that first night, 3,000 or so screaming Brussels women. No Finnish pickets out front, thank God!

Ernie had called in sick. I knew he'd holed up in his hotel room bed with two chicks he'd picked up from the rave club in town the previous evening while Brent and I were nixing nicotine.

Cody took over the master of ceremonies duties, and his understudy, Larry, took over Ernie's "Apocalypse Now" and biker numbers. Even though Ernie's absence screwed up their normal routines, Cody and Larry enjoyed the change of pace from monotonous scenes repeated each night. With the exception of Russell, the leads were understudies for one another, rehearsing each other's numbers in case of emergency. Russell never had emergencies. He wasn't about to allow anyone to take over his envied star position.

Everything went smoothly until the biker number midway through the second act. I was in the wings ready for my turn on stage, also curious to see how Larry's energy might affect the small production number.

One problem existed. Larry hadn't rehearsed riding on stage like Brando on a Harley-Davidson. His entrance wearing leather biker gear, permanently-curled hair draped over his shoulders, was a good deal less than grand. He made it to center stage all right, shoved the kickstand down with his right foot, then continued to rev the motor so much that Darrell and Robert, the other strip leads already standing in front of their Harleys, couldn't hear the music. This was typical of Larry, garnering all the attention from the audience. The revving engine did the trick.

Inability to hear the beat screwed up the other guys' moves. Darrell was furious, anger contorting his expression. After all, he was the rhythm king, as witnessed with Christina that sex-filled night in Stockholm. He kept staring Larry down as he lip-synced the original song and twisted the handlebar as though he were tightening a bolt with a wrench.

The smoky exhaust, hell-bent toward stage left, was spuming into Darrell's face. He started choking, then coughing while backing up. He shouted to me standing in the wings. "Tell him to shut his fuckin' engine down!"

I started waving my arms at Larry. Didn't work. Larry was on a personal high, smiling at the audience, baring those perfect teeth like King Kong with Fay Wray within his reach, gyrating on the Harley seat, and repeatedly punching the air with a fist.

Finally, Darrell could take no more. He danced in front of Larry, gave him a gentle shove, and yelled, "Shut off—" The words were lost for the moment as the planned pyro exploded all over the stage.

Larry was so startled by Darrell's unplanned arrival in his line of vision and the exploding fireworks surrounding him that he fell backward off the Harley, giving his hand on the handlebar another twist to the right.

What does a gunning motorcycle do when suddenly out of control?

Oh God no!

It jumped toward the edge of the stage and the front rows of the audience. Darrell leapt for the machine quicker than a dirt biker flying into the void over a hill, grabbed a handlebar, and diverted the machine off stage right.

A large crash came from backstage as the Harley hit the far theater wall, sputtered, and died.

Larry, bless his professional heart, was lying in the middle of the stage floor, groping for his dropped mike prop, not knowing what the hell had happened. The music boomed on. So did the pyro. By God, the prop man wasn't about to stop his blasting best for anything. He'd had enough of Ernie's wrath over his own personal war number to singe his butt hairs.

Larry picked up the sync in mid-lip and sang on without the mike. Have you ever tried to pick up a lyric somewhere in the middle? Not easy. At least it was recorded. Larry continued on bravely, working into the dance routine Darrell and Robert had resumed.

I think the audience thought it was all a put-on, and cheered their every movement.

Larry had to improvise the rest of the number, since he didn't have the parked bike to strip next to. It called for slipping and sliding over and around the bike seat while taking everything off down to the thong, then a complete strip with backside to the audience. His motions were perfect ad-lib. I recognized the movements from his starring number in the Hotel Chippendale scene. The audience didn't seem to recognize the repeat from the first act. They were more interested in his crotch. He turned around and threw his thong stage right as the lights blacked out.

The Harley, pride lost backstage, had only a dented front fender to its credit. And Larry had added an original number to his.

Everyone was too chicken to tell Ernie what had happened during his precious bike scene that night. The crew even replaced the Harley fender the next day, so that he wouldn't find out.

We were all mistaken — one look at the new fender and Ernie was all over the crew about why it had been replaced.

Someone ratted.

I was in the dressing room when Ernie stormed in with fire in his eyes and vengeance in his fist. "Larry, what the fuck did you do to my number last night?"

Uh-oh! I'd better get out of here pronto, I decided. Ernie's formidable frame blocked the doorway. Long black hair shook across his naked, hairless shoulders. His eyes were vampire-intense.

Larry pushed back his chair and stood. "Just a dumb mistake, Ernie. I'm not a biker. Didn't quite get the hang of—"

"From what I hear, you screwed up my entire number. How could you do a stupid damn thing like that?"

I put my two cents worth in. "Ernie, Larry handled it really well. The audience didn't even—"

"Who asked you, fuckface? This is between Larry and me."

"But—"

"Butt out."

I remained quiet. It wasn't my problem after all.

Ernie blustered, "No more. You are not my understudy anymore, Larry."

Larry was fuming now. "Who the hell made you God? The job's already taken."

Ernie headed for Larry. I stepped in between. "Calm down, Ernie. It was just a mistake. They happen all the time in the show and you know it."

"Shut up, Troy."

Larry added fuel to the flame. "If you'd stop fuckin' around all night instead of doin' the show like you're supposed to, it wouldn't have happened. It's your own fault, Ernie."

I managed to back Ernie toward the door. "Look, you guys, Mark is out on the stage. He'll be back here any second. You don't want him to hear this."

Ernie dropped his hands. "Good. I sure as hell want to talk to him."

I spoke up again. "Not a good idea, Ernie. He was really pissed when you didn't show up last night. I'd let it drop if I were you."

The words took the wind out of Ernie's sails. He came about, deflating his anger spinnaker. "You're on my shit list, Larry." He stormed out of the dressing room. "You, too, Troy."

Of course, Ernie didn't say anything to Mark Pakin. Couldn't afford to. Everything blew over in the next few days. Larry and Ernie were soon snorting lines of coke again together as if nothing had happened.

I, for one, thought the runaway bike should have been written into the scene and featured on the billboard out front.

Fantastic show business, throwing fear into all those brassy gals out front. The result of such excitement during a performance should never be underestimated.

After the show that evening, Larry and I went to the after-hours, stage-announced disco bar, Mirano Continental, the smartest dance venue in Brussels where the young and hip admired each other and themselves. We laughed all the way there over the bike scene. We even joked about Ernie's fit of temper.

A couple of hours later, we had dates from Mirano. They spoke only Dutch. Thirty minutes of gestures and winks and the message came through loud and clear where their interest lay. A dangled key held not so subtly in front of our faces called for tricks with the chicks.

Since our hotel was a good distance away, their local flat at two-thirty in the morning seemed the perfect solution. Surely my girl had two bedrooms. If not, the living room floor would suffice nicely.

We were on.

A couple of blocks in the cold night air, and I was ready for a little warmth — no, a lot of warmth.

"Larry! How far away you think she lives?"

"Better be soon. I'm freezing my ass off. My curls are turning into icicles."

My girl stopped at a storefront door. Nondescript drapes covered the plate glass windows on the inside.

I asked Larry, "What does the neon sign say?"

"Fuck if I know."

"You live here?" I asked.

She nodded, opened the door, and led us in.

We stood in the plush foyer of a fitness center, an expensive place with Jean-Claude Van Damme pictures plastered on the walls.

Inside, more Van Damme photos. Everywhere. It was a huge three-story place with enough equipment to turn everyone in Brussels into Mr. Belgians. It was either owned by Jean-Claude or he trained there when visiting his hometown.

My date pulled me over to the far wall like she owned the place, took a tumble mat down, and ripped off her leather jacket, blouse, and jeans. Her muscles had muscles, and her breasts were small with large nipples, a real taste treat. I was ready to dive in when she started pulling at my shirt buttons.

I still hadn't understood a word she'd spoken. Her gestures, however, were golden. She was on her hands and knees in seconds, and I was fucking her from behind soon after that.

I was just getting into my stride when Larry strolled over, barefoot, stripped to his bikini underwear. "You got a rubber, buddy?"

Tina pulled off me, obviously embarrassed by nudity and our activity. Didn't bother me. Of course, she didn't understand Larry's question.

"Jean pocket." I laughed.

He found one and took off.

Our sex wasn't too wild, just straight-out fucking sans the refinements I'd perfected on tour.

The erotic sounds spoken in a different language turned me on. I wondered what she was saying between moans.

My home run came almost my first time at bat. Her sensuous inner muscle control must have had something to do with it.

We dressed, then went up the steps to another part of the gym. We sat on the stairs halfway up and smoked a joint. She started grabbing my crotch again, and we ended up fucking a second time right there. She must have thought my body was flubber the way she squeezed me with those powerful thighs. I had a new insight into the benefits of muscle build-up.

The second time took longer. I wasn't sure she climaxed when I did, and didn't care. We pulled our clothes on again, then headed up to the suntanning floor.

I couldn't believe my eyes. Larry was fucking his girl in a suntan bed, lid up. I wished for Ernie's video camera. What a dynamite scene that would have made on the bus VCR. I could visualize the sub-title: Vampire fangs his way into new territories.

We left them singeing the suntanning bed with herculean effort, then headed back down the stairs to smoke another joint. This naturally led to a third inning. She liked it straight, but rough. I made a three-base hit. Must have had to do with all that night training from Eileen in Copenhagen.

Larry and I finally finished our exercising romp, thanked Claude's photos, and waved goodbye. We never knew their names and never saw them again. I decided I'd have to look into exercise techniques when I got back home.

16

The last week of April, our second week in Belgium, we were on a bus once more, heading north to Europe's largest seaport and home of the European diamond trade. Chippendales had scheduled us for two shows in Antwerp.

I was sitting by myself, in my usual seat on the left side of the bus. Larry sat just in front of me next to Scott. He usually sat in the back with the rest of the leads. Larry wasn't exactly a fraternal fellow. For that reason, his following was minuscule. Mostly me. Even though I knew he was trouble, I befriended him. Always felt sorry for anyone left out of conversations most of the time. I didn't realize his loner attitude was by choice.

Mark Pakin said on the mike up front, "Listen, men. I have a story for you." He proceeded to tell us about a Chip from last year's tour group who got busted for trafficking in counterfeit Belgian francs. He was still in prison in Brussels. He added a warning about anyone getting involved with anybody offering money deals. "Bad stuff. Lots of it over here. Be careful."

Scott said quietly to Larry, "Shit! Told you these hot francs were nothing but trouble. Too good a deal. We gotta get rid of them quick."

Larry leaned closer to Scott. "Relax, man. Don't do nothin' crazy. I told you I got a source in Antwerp to launder it. Twenty percent of face."

I was not surprised that money-hungry Larry, who liked to gamble more than anyone I ever knew, was involved in dangerous shit. He was always into something. If it was illegal, all the better.

Larry and I were sitting in the hotel bar the afternoon before our first Antwerp show, having a dark beer. The other Chips had left one by one to look around the seaport city or whatever. We had leisure time to burn before dinner at the theater that night.

Larry suggested we check out the porno peep show place across the street from our theater.

"Peep show? Come on! You aren't serious?"

"Sure, man. Bet you five bucks the girls are young and juicy."

I laughed. "Every time I think you're the shallowest person I ever met, you always manage to take a little more out of the pool."

"Troy, come on. It'll be a kick."

"In that flea-infested trap? No way! The only kick you'll get is an unwanted itch in the balls."

"I got one already. I wanna see how they do it."

"Do what?"

"Ya know. Strip and stuff."

I sighed. "What the hell! But I'm not staying if it's too raunchy." Guess I wanted to be talked into it. If I needed an excuse, a fiver was now at stake.

I knew when we entered the joint that this was a dim-witted idea. The smelly place made garbage smell like perfume.

After exchanging guilders for tokens, we walked into one of the darkened booths, boot soles sticking on the floor with each step. It was the type of place with glass show windows where a screen rolls up on the inside and you can watch girls live, doing a diddling dare deal for the darlings out dere — boys, or girls, I suppose. Girls live. Barely!

You know, the overripe aroma of too many doses of Lysol. In this case, too little, and the typical type of stripper: haggard with drooping tits and enough make-up to turn a drag queen jealous. Worn-out, over-the-hill types, for sure.

A box of tissue was mounted on the wall to the right. Two chrome chairs with slit vinyl seats even Goodwill wouldn't have accepted lounged uninvitingly in front of the window. I wouldn't have sat in one even to watch Sharon Stone spread her legs.

After Larry deposited several tokens, the shade rose

to reveal a young girl, looking newly off the boat from Amsterdam, sucking on a cigarette, lying on a sagging bed. A light flashed a couple of times, alerting her she had a customer. She looked lazily at the window, pulled off her flimsy negligee to reveal her nudity, except for pasties with tassels attached on her perky boobs, very little makeup, hardly haggard — definitely under the hill. Couldn't have been more than 18 years old.

I laughed and handed Larry a fiver.

With a wink toward the window, she started the bump and grind Antwerp-style, a bit unsure of herself.

She was a mechanical doll, all wound up and ready to writhe home. Jerky movements. Tassels twirling dangerously, threatening to slap her face.

She was built like a Dutch windmill, top-heavy, with tassels twirling like Don Quixote's sword. She reminded me of a girl playing a stripper who was having trouble finding something to take off. She smiled nervously and moved closer to the window. Her fingers moved south. The manual must have said that's what you did next.

As she got closer to the window, tongue out, ready to lick the glass, she suddenly looked startled. She stopped her tongue mid-swipe, straightened, then pointed at us, shrieking, "Chippendales . . . Chippendales!"

In seconds, all the other strippers in the room came running to see us, including a naked guy. They'd no doubt left disappointed customers halfway to orgasm city, just to ogle us.

Half of them wore those pink peek-a-boo negligees, the other half, boos on display. The guy wore only a cock-ring around his balls and a big drooping dick. Something for everybody!

Talk about a reverse show. They stared at us as if we were the animals in the cage. Bizarre!

The guy said with a deep voice into a mike, "We see you show. Fabulous!" He said the word as if a recent addition to his English vocabulary. "Fabulous," he repeated for emphasis.

The girls chimed in, laughing and squealing in Dutch with an occasional "Fabulous," only it came out more like "fab-lus." I recognized the Dutch language now, having heard it all evening in my favorite fitness gym in Brussels.

Larry and I looked at each other and laughed. "Mirror, mirror on the wall, who's the sexiest of 'em all?"

The naked guy, short and skinny to the point of emaciation, took charge of the group, speaking broken English, probably the only one who could. "Come on . . . show all. Private. The strip." He punched one of the girls on the arm, said something in Dutch, and pointed toward the back of the room.

I found myself saying, "No . . . no. We came to see your show." I pointed at the young girl, face lit up like a virgin on wedding night.

They didn't understand what I was saying. At least

I was flattered the six girls remembered who the hell I was.

Our show music suddenly erupted from the speaker above us: "Drift Away." Apparently, someone had bought the cassette tape in the theater lobby the night before.

"Strip . . . strip! Fab-lus," The girls picked up the guy's words.

Larry looked at me and smiled, then said the now infamous words, "Why not?" Larry, the nymphomaniac of our group, was always game to drop his drawers for a good cause — even a bad cause. He fluffed his long curly blond hair, ready and waiting for me to make a first move.

I stared at him, incredulous, then laughed. "I don't strip!"

Larry was already moving his hips to the beat. "Okay. You sing. I strip."

"You're not really going to—"

He was already taking off his leather jacket an arm at a time, twirling and wiggling to the beat, really into it from the get-go.

Can you imagine anything more weird? Larry peeling off his T-shirt with practiced skill, shifting his boots on the sticky floor, me half laughing, half lip-syncing my number. We were performing in front of a chorus of naked sex-show freaks a few feet away on the other side of a plate glass window, cheering and stamping their feet like football fans.

Larry timed his strip with the music and was down to his thong bikini in two minutes flat.

The girls' tassels were swinging in sympathy, all except our new girl who kept slapping herself with them. The young man was erect, playing with himself. When I say erect, this guy gave the term new meaning. Big as a California cucumber.

As we headed toward the finish, there was no stopping Larry. He was really into it now, sporting a woody as well. The ladies (I use the term loosely) were shrieking and yelling in Dutch, and pointing at the tool tenting Larry's thong.

The man on the inside yelled, "All . . . naked, all . . . naked, all . . . naked!" as he whipped himself into a frenzy. The chorus tuned in. "All . . . naked, all . . . naked."

Larry obliged. With slow, teasing movements, he undid the Velcro strips on each side of his protruding thong, held the slim piece of fabric over his crotch (actually, it held itself), then turned the other cheeks to the window before dropping the thong to the floor.

Cheers erupted like loud stage pyro blasts.

As the music faded, I sighed. Thank God! Number over.

But Larry wasn't finished. He turned around and began jacking off to the delight of a different kind of squealing audience. The girls were in a fingering frenzy.

Here I was again in a situation I felt totally embarrassed and stupid about. No more!

I yanked the door open and ran down the hall and out into the street, music strains of my own voice still ringing in my ear.

I was sober, yet wearing the moral cloak of a curious voyeur. What was I doing in this erotic hell? How low had I sunk? I had a headache. I felt nauseous. I was trembling with shame. Disgusted!

With Larry? With the sex-show perverts?

No.

Myself!

I walked in the cool spring air for several blocks, not knowing where I was going. Not caring. How much more degradation was I going to involve myself in? It wasn't as if I hadn't agreed to go into Sleaze Hell. Did I have any dignity left at all?

Not much!

Four months of booze and broads had taken their toll. My mind had dropped below the belt. How did I get into this mess in my life anyway? I was on a lark, doing what I pleased, without regard to the consequences, not caring about anyone except numero uno. How many people in life can sustain this kind of shit without realizing what such debauchery does to the mind? The words "dope, booze, broads" kept ringing in my feeble mind. What was I going to do about it?

At dinner backstage that night in Antwerp, I managed to fend off Larry's questions as to "What happened to you, man? You didn't stay for the big finish.

The guy on the other side and I whitewashed the window, both sides."

I blurted a feeble excuse, "Got sick to my stomach. Had to get away from that putrid smell."

That was partly the truth. The consummate segment, though, was the need to get away from myself.

Nobody was twisting my arm, saying, "You have to do everything to the fullest, regardless of how degrading, just for the experience."

It was all my own undoing. "Why not?" wasn't working for me anymore.

17

Two days after our People Peep Show, the troupe headed north to Amsterdam for a one-night stand. We were to complete the last night of a ten-day engagement for Chippendale tour group three, which was moving across the English Channel to perform at the Strand during a two-month stay in London.

The countryside through southern Holland was spring green. Earth dikes held back the ocean from the extended flatland. Windmills, the power source for pumping water into fields full of thousands of tulips in bloom, were sprinkled picturesquely across the landscape.

This city of 1,001 bridges was combed with a latticework of rivers and canals, the largest being the North Sea Canal which joined the Ij River in central Amsterdam.

The new guys wanted to see Crooked Street in

Voorburgwal, Amsterdam's world-famous red-light district. We headed across a labyrinth of canals and through winding streets and grand boulevards until we arrived at a cobblestone street. It seemed a contradiction that the Dutch, noted for strict morality verging on puritanism, were also stern upholders of absolute personal freedoms. This belief was authorization aplenty for the red light district around Rembrandtsplein.

The winding streets were choked with sex clubs, topless bars, bawdy nightclubs, and a rash of porno shops. Well-lit plate glass windows framed busty females — some beckoning, some yawning, one idly painting her nails, and one who shouted at us, "Hello, Yankees," trying to entice the horny inside. Believe me, I'd had enough of such fare in Antwerp. I wanted out of the place.

Because Cody and I were low on grass, he pulled me aside. "Come on, Troy. I know just the spot to get pot. Cheap, too."

Cody with his black eyes and angular cheekbones looked like a young Gregory Peck on steroids. He was Jewish, non-practicing, existing on drugs — so many that it was a wonder they hadn't killed him yet. He dropped acid, smoked pot like a fiend, did Ecstasy, and snorted lines of coke, all the time. He seemed to function in the show only when he was high on something. Imagine what he could have done sober.

He'd already confided in me that his parents had thrown him out of the house when he was 17 because of his pot habit. He didn't even finish high school. His parents never once tried to help him by getting him to drug rehab. He'd shamed the family. One doesn't do that in a Jewish household.

At this point, I doubted rehab would have done much good. He was too far gone. He seemed proud of his ability to maintain while he was turned on. What a joke! No one ever truly knew the real Cody, except maybe anxious drug dealers all over Scandinavia.

He'd gotten an interview with the Chippendales due to his spectacular looks and body tone. Imagine someone so wiped out all the time, even having a body to tone. He did though, enough so to be a Chippendale. He *was* a good dancer. Even had a fair-to-middling singing voice. I wondered why he never took girls back to the rooms at night like the rest of us. We always left him in the club of the evening, doing drugs and a frantic fandango in the middle of an appreciative crowd.

Cody took me down another winding street and into a drugstore in Voorburgwal. I use the term "drugstore" literally. The front windows were small and inconspicuous. I didn't understand the Dutch name above the door.

We entered what appeared to be a cafe with clean white walls, polished wood peg floor, and antique-looking wooden tables and chairs. The overpowering melange of hash and marijuana aromas smacked me in the nose, right off.

The few patrons were actually sitting at the tables imbibing. A couple of guys were passing back and forth a water bong. Another three were sharing Thai sticks. This was a Dutch version of an Oriental opium den.

A very long counter, chest high, stretched halfway to the end of the long, narrow room. Cody pointed to the dark green padded stools. "Take a seat over there."

A middle-aged man, pulling at his heavy beard, sauntered over, took one look at us, and handed us a menu written in English.

"Shit! You got to be kidding!" This was unlike any menu I'd ever seen. All the entries were drugs, listed in alphabetical order down the left side of the page, with amounts in guilders under the word "cost" in the far right-hand column. Several categories of hashish, marijuana from around the world, cocaine, heroin, opium, Ecstasy, acid, and an entire roster of drugs I'd never even heard of. Everyone's choice of poison, all merchandised in neat little rows, all designed to maim the mind.

I glanced around to see if the Dutch police were looking over our shoulders.

Cody laughed at my expression. "Dynamite place, right?"

I began to sweat, thinking the den could be raided by the bears any minute. I preferred to hibernate.

Cody assured me everything was cool. "You wanted pot. They got pot. Cheap, too. Just look at these prices."

I thought I'd become a liberal thinker by now. Guess

I wasn't ready for this kind of emporium. An over-the-counter drugstore like this in the U.S. would have put street dealers out of business permanently. Interesting thought.

We made our purchase in guilders and left, none too soon for me.

That night in Amsterdam at the Muziek, the most beautiful theater we played on tour, the show went especially well. The audience seemed more appreciative than usual. The shrillness of female voices echoed throughout the ornately gilded theater, a little more "girlsterous" than usual.

My favorite number in the show, because it featured yours truly, was the one just before the finale.

The number started with Brent entering stage right singing "End of the Road." A blue spot followed him to center stage. Then I entered stage right singing the second phrase and stood next to him.

By this time in the show, the audience recognized favorite cast members the minute they appeared on stage. My walk to center was accompanied by cheers and applause. I weighed how well I'd done in each night's performance by the audience response during the number. This night in Amsterdam it was extra heavy. I sort of choked my way through one of the lyric phrases, emotion suddenly hitting me. I was overly vulnerable tonight for some reason.

Then Harold, our black dancer, entered stage left,

singing. He was very popular with audiences. Had a strong baritone voice best suited to musical comedy. Finally, Ernie entered through the back curtains, making our foursome complete.

Once we were spaced equidistant at the front, each with our own mike and blue spot, harmonizing on the R&B-style song, the audience quieted, almost reverently. The ladies in the front row began to light candles individually. One by one, the rest of the audience followed suit. Flickering light moved front to back like waves rushing toward a distant shore.

Tonight, the twinkling lights were sweeter than Dutch chocolate. A beautiful sight from the stage, inspiring me especially, as though everyone was present just for me. I felt I was more than a singer in a male strip show. I was in show business, making my mark in the world, and the world was paying attention. Illusion is a wondrous thing, the essence of which dreams are filled. This candle-lighting ritual had followed us throughout the tour. It was the only number in which the crowd hung on the music and lyrics without clapping and shouting for everyone to take it all off.

I took the lead melody while the other three slid into back-up mode. I felt myself soar into the high notes, sliding up and down the scale to the lower register. I was suddenly back at Cafe DaVinci's in Kirkland, pouring my heart into a karaoke mike, feeling lonely, abandoned, hoping there was a better life for me somewhere out there.

My enthusiasm was infectious. The back-up guys were soon on the same high, inspiring me into improvisation at a new level.

I stepped back into the final harmony until the music ended.

Then deafening silence.

The crowd was on its feet like a shot, yelling, holding candles high. They extinguished them, then began to applaud and whistle like never before. Then stage blackout.

Tears were running unashamedly down my cheeks. We'd never had an ovation like that. I felt, selfishly, it was mostly for me.

The other guys were slapping me on the back. "Great stuff, Troy." "Fantastic." "What got into you, man?"

I couldn't even speak. I just nodded and moved off stage right. Had to be alone with my musical metaphors.

The next morning around nine, the phone rang in my Caranza Crest Hotel room near the theater district.

I yawned awake. Who could be calling this early? I glanced over at Brent's empty bed, heard the shower running, then reached for the phone receiver. "Hello?"

A woman's husky, low-pitched voice replied, "Is this Troy Kline?"

"Yeah."

"Are you the singer from the Chippendale show at the Muziek Theater?"

"Uh, who wants to know?"

"Oh. Sorry. I'm Sarah Prentice. I saw your show last night and—"

"How did you get my number?" I sighed. Another groupie! This one sounded older than most.

"The hotel operator. Please don't hang up. I'm sure you get calls from ladies all the time. I have a proposition for you."

Oh boy! Here we go. "Does it involve sex? If it does, I—"

She laughed, a deep, throaty chuckle, designed to disarm. "No, no. Nothing like that. I'm a film producer."

Bells began to ring. I threw back the covers and slid my feet to the floor. "Did you say fi . . . fi . . . film producer?"

"Yes. I'm making an American suspense film here in Amsterdam, and I'd like to talk to you about a small part in it."

Hallelujah! My ship was arriving at the North Sea Canal docks. Wait a minute! Ernie was probably behind this elaborate scheme to get even with me for getting even with him. "Is this some sort of joke?"

"I assure you it is not, Mr. Kline. I was at the Chippendale show last night and especially loved your number near the end. The one with the candles."

" 'End Of The Road'?"

"Yes, that's the one. I was very impressed with your

voice and style. We have a nightclub scene that occurs at Club Cellar in the red-light district here in Amsterdam. I need a fresh face and voice in a musical background number for a scene with our star. I'd like you to audition for the part."

I was ready to say, "You're kidding!" Thank God, my wits surfaced just in time. "It would have to be today. Ah . . . this morning in fact. The cast and crew are heading back to Brussels this afternoon." Damn! Here I was demanding without thinking. I must sound like a complete idiot.

"That could be arranged. How about eleven o'clock at my hotel?"

Uh-oh! Her hotel. This *was* Ernie's boomerang joke.

She must have caught my hesitation. "We have a rehearsal room booked here on the mezzanine. I'll have a piano brought in. Shall we say eleven this morning then?"

I looked up. Brent was standing in the doorway with a towel hugging his waist, listening.

"That will be fine. See you soon, Miss—"

"Prentice. Sarah Prentice."

"Thank you."

I hung up, looked at Brent, and started laughing. I told him all about the conversation, ending with, "Ernie must have put one of his Dutch babes up to it. He's probably laughing his head off about now."

Brent shook his head, "I don't think so, Troy. I'd go along with it if I were you. What have you got to lose?"

I shook my head. "Nothing but a lot of razzing, I guess."

Sarah Prentice, an attractive forty or so executive type in a smart tweed pantsuit and no makeup, was for real. She greeted me in the Savoy Room of the Amsterdam Marriott Hotel precisely at eleven. She was a tall lady, wearing a commanding mantle suitable to her stature. Her brunette hair was too long for someone her age.

Everything she had said on the phone turned out to be legitimate. *Dutch Treat* was the tentative title for an independent studio film starring some young new body-building karate type named Lance Billings, whom I'd never heard of. It was about a diamond heist, with lots of twists and turns in the plot.

That was enough information for me. Because I didn't have musical arrangements for a pianist, I'd brought along my cassette player with a tape of the background music for "Unchained Melody," my lucky song I'd used to audition for the Chippendales.

An hour later, I had the job. The good part was that I would be paid well for a few hours' work, my hotel room for two more nights in Amsterdam, and airfare to Brussels two days hence.

I signed a release contract for work to be performed and was told I'd be given a check for three grand after I'd completed filming. Fantastic! It was a month's pay with the show — for one day's work, plus my big chance in a movie. Some big recording studio exec would see me in it and give me a contract to make my first CD. My dream was coming true.

Sarah Prentice had already arranged for the scene to be shot the next evening in Club Cellar, since it was a Monday and the night spot would be closed until Tuesday evening. The director had planned to have the house band perform a number and dub in different music with a different singer back in a Hollywood studio.

After seeing me perform, she switched plans, saying I would add more authenticity to the scene. The director had agreed.

The timing couldn't have been better since we had the next two nights off before appearing for a few more shows in Brussels.

I made all the arrangements with Mark Pakin. Hooray for Hollywood! I was on my way. My funk disappeared with the next morning's fog. I couldn't believe my good fortune. I was being discovered all over again, being appreciated for my singing ability.

My great news, thanks to Brent, spread through the Chips like vanilla in a latte, sweeter with the tasting.

Everyone congratulated me before getting on the bus. Brent pulled me back just before boarding. "Good luck with your big break, Troy. You deserve it."

Those words meant more than any I'd heard on the whole tour. I expected Ernie to say words of encouragement to me. He didn't. Maybe he hadn't heard.

I had thought recording was a great high. Appearing in a full-length film, even though it was just one scene, would be like standing on top of the Matterhorn.

By ten the next morning, I was heading into Voorburgwal searching out Club Cellar for rehearsals. Would you believe, they decided to let me do my audition number, "Unchained Melody." Of course, all I had was my karaoke tape. They even agreed to use it for the filming. They would get the necessary release permission back home.

Because I was unavailable for rehearsals, I was told a local band would fill in a special arrangement later. Apparently, this sort of dubbing was standard procedure in films.

I had visions of this beautiful nightclub with flowing drapes bordering the stage, and a sophisticated audience dressed in furs and tuxedos. In Voorburgwal? Get real, Troy!

Club Cellar was a Bette Davis, "what-a-dump" conundrum.

In the daylight, the place looked like a run-down version of the peep show hell Larry and I had visited in Antwerp. It was billed out front as a topless club. Had to be some reason for people to frequent this derelict's dive. The grungy floor, not yet cleaned from the Sunday night crowd, smelled like a ripe kitty-litter box.

The walls were bright purple, draped with hideous abstract murals so bizarre that Salvador Dali would have thrown up. My fantasy dream street had turned into nightmare alley; however, seeing all the filming equipment near the raised portion at the end of the room got me excited.

Five black musicians, obviously members of a combo, sat hungover-looking on the platform (one could hardly call it a stage). Keyboard, drums, bass, and two electric guitars surrounded them. A small, dingy sign stated "The Raisins."

I introduced myself.

"Troy Kline, from the U.S." I stuck out a hand. No hands were forthcoming.

They nodded. I withdrew my hand. Cool!

I seemed to be the only one nervous about this film bit. I tried again, "Pretty great, huh, being in a movie?"

A couple of nods. They didn't understand a word. "No Englisa," one of them managed.

The assistant director, Hans something, recruited from Amsterdam, finally spoke to me in accented English. He repeated the words in Dutch for the members of the combo. "Gentlemen, I'll need for you to run through the song a couple of times so I can set the lights and camera angles. Roy, I'd like you to—"

"Troy."

"Yes. Well, Troy, you'll be center stage with a handmike." He shouted behind him, "Someone get this guy a hand-mike." He turned back to me. "The spots will be on you, so don't move around. Just do the number, looking around at an imaginary audience. Not too much animation, right? Right."

He turned to a flunky and pointed. "Ditch that stupid Raisins sign, Sean."

And so it went. The band rehearsed, playing an ad-lib version of my cassette recording, so their hand and body movements would be in sync with my voice. They sounded like an out-of-tune version of a burlesque show band. I seemed to be the only one who cared about their lack of musical ability. What did I expect in a topless bar in the red-light district of Amsterdam? Thank God, the actual music arrangement would be dubbed in back in Hollywood by a professional group.

Around one o'clock, we tried our first take. Two stagehands came out with canisters resembling fire extinguishers and sprayed smoke everywhere. Atmosphere! Can't have a nightclub without cigarette smoke. Can't be a nightclub without an audience, either. Yet ours was as empty as a cemetery at midnight.

They'd dub in the crowd later.

What about nightclub sounds? Dub it in later. Music, crowd, sound? Dub it later. The only thing authentic was the stench of the place. It was hard to get inspired with all this make-believe, standing in front of beady-eyed cameras with a lousy back-up band that should have been further back — like maybe in Helsinki. I was getting a headache.

We started. I coughed my way through the first take. Too much smoke! "Sorry. Let me try it again."

Once the smoke level was corrected, I performed what I thought to be a reasonably good number.

"Cut! Cut!" Hans shouted. "Roy, sorry, my man, but your arm is swimming all over the place. Switch hands with the mike every few phrases. Need more animation. And turn your head more to the right. It's your best profile."

"You said you didn't want much animation."

"Yeah? Well, I don't want a zombie either. Somewhere between zombie and Michael Jackson, right?"

"Uh, sure."

"And for Christ's sake, calm down. No more swimming. This isn't the English Channel."

I wasn't surprised at my movements. My nerves were a jangle of Jello. I was sweating, ruining the makeup that had been applied by a lady well over sixty.

Hans, having taken notice, said, "And someone fix the rivers on Roy's face. Make it quick. We don't have all day."

"Troy," I said feebly.

Five minutes later, after a makeup mop-up, a prop man wearing a headphone set moved forward. "Take two. Nightclub scene. *Dutch Treat*." He snapped the clip of the small chalkboard downward. Every time he did that, I jumped.

"Action." Hans pointed at me.

Ten takes later, my scene was "in the can" as they say in film lingo. I expected at least a "Thank you, that was great, Mr. Kline," from the assistant director, or a

"Join us for a celebration drink at the hotel, Mr. Kline."

Hans's sally consisted of "We're through with you now, Roy."

That's it? Fucker didn't even get my name right.

He said something in Dutch to the band boys, obviously dismissing them as well.

"Everybody, kill the lights. Let's get out of this shit hole."

I thought about asking the Raisins to join me for a drink or whatever, even though they didn't speak English. Before I got to it, they were gone, leaving their instruments enclosed in cases with enough tape holding them together to place them in the mummy hall of fame. They were the group working the gig here every night.

The Raisins and this dump deserved each other.

I couldn't believe it. It was nine p.m. We'd been at it all day, for one little scene, which would probably be cut into with some sort of Lance Billings emoting action out in the nightclub audience. I hadn't even met the star or any other actors in the film, only Sarah Prentice, Hans something, and the makeup lady. Didn't even properly meet the members of the band.

After picking up my check, I headed back to the Caranza Crest for a lonely night, dreaming of film stardom in the not-too-distant future. Couldn't sleep. That wasn't so unusual. I was up most nights, drinking or fucking. Why should tonight be any different? It was. I was all alone!

I tossed and turned, and finally zonked out about five a.m.

The next morning, I was smart enough to mail my check for $3,000 to my Issaquah, Washington, bank. If I cashed it here, I'd have spent it stupidly. Probably on pot.

Sometimes, I had common sense.

My brain was ticking far too much lately, turning inner thoughts over and over in my mind like a clothes washer on spin cycle that never stopped. I was getting sick of this fast-paced living. If that wasn't enough, I was playing a new role called "wishful thinking" about film stardom. My ego was pushing ahead like a runaway Seattle waterfront trolley charging down the track with only Elliott Bay in front.

Back in Brussels, I bragged to everyone who would listen about the set, the cameras, and the action of *Dutch Treat*, stretching the limit to being buddy-buddy with the star of the movie, having a few drinks with him after the shoot, smoking pot with the band, etc. What did they know? They weren't there.

My intent was to make everyone jealous. I think I succeeded. Some of the Chips were down.

I really became obnoxious. Sarcastic remarks, most of them unkind to people, erupted like snake's venom, poisoning my reason. I was soon arguing with everyone, rattling my tail over stupid slights and insignificant incidents.

I never used to be that way. What was happening to me?

I had to get a hold of myself.

The morning after my return to Brussels, Mark held a staff meeting in the hotel wait room at eleven a.m. The meeting was a director's warning lecture about bad attitudes. I guess it wasn't just me with all the tension building. The disease was spreading as if being an asshole was suddenly the rage.

Something Mark said, clearly singling me out, set me off. I stood, shook my head, and started to walk out. He yelled at me to get back there. It was the first time I'd ever heard him raise his voice.

I turned back, gave him more attitude, and kept on going. After all, I was a film star now.

After my stupid exit during an important meeting, things got decidedly worse between Mark and myself. It was not a good idea to piss off the boss. But when you're young, the world owes you a living, not the other way around.

If I were to run across Mark Pakin today, I'd apologize for my actions throughout the tour. They were totally uncalled for. I had become what I disliked about some of the leads, a pompous jerk. "I'm a singing star; the show can't do without me" thoughts completely blindsided me.

I was emulating Ernie's attitudes, but there was a big difference between the two of us. He was a well-paid lead; I was a flunky at the bottom of the pay scale, a singer who thought much too highly of himself.

But all that was going to change, wasn't it? Just wait until *Dutch Treat* was released in the United States sometime in the fall. I'd be an overnight sensation.

18

The first week of May 1993, the sun finally showered our world for awhile. Springtime in Brussels. There must be a song lyric somewhere in that line. The spectacular weather affected us all, adding a warmth, a spring to our dance steps. I could actually wear a muscle shirt around the city without a jacket or sweater.

At the start of the second week, we had another couple of days off before heading into Germany for two nights in Dusseldorf.

Ernie and Darrell talked Mark Pakin into letting us take our bus to Paris to visit one of the other two Chippendale tour groups. The Number Two traveling circus was doing two weeks in the heart of Paris. Research on how other Chips performed would help us all do a better job in our own show.

Mark went along with the idea, even encouraged us in our endeavor. We had to behave ourselves in

Paris though, and not give Mike, the bus driver, any lip.

Yeah, right! Telling this group to behave ourselves was like waving tits in our face and saying these are for nursing babies only.

"And no drugs crossing the border. The French guards don't take kindly to anyone carrying. They aren't as lenient as the Belgians. Remember, they don't much like Americans to begin with. Believe me, guys, you'll end up in prison if you get caught smuggling anything."

I nudged Cody, "Is he for real? Even pot?"

"Don't worry about it. I know how to do it."

I shook my head. Even though we'd all done it crossing borders throughout Scandinavia, Mark had never warned us before. No way was I going to tempt fate.

I was excited about this side trip into France. Imagine — Paris, the Eiffel Tower, the Arc de Triomphe, Champs Elysées, not to mention French cooking.

The City of Light was reportedly one of the most beautiful cities in the world. Even my ambitious show business plans as a kid in Wenatchee never included Paris, France.

The trip south was uneventful, even crossing the border, until we came down into a valley into the city of Lille, France. It was a beautiful town tucked away into foothills like some fantasy village in one of Rene's *Once Upon a Time* books, as we used to call them. I wished my daughter could have been here to see it.

Sidewalk cafes dominated the cobblestone streets in the center of town. Geraniums and petunias bloomed extravagantly in hanging baskets along the main street in the bright noontime sun, adding to garlic aromas drifting along the boulevard. Trees were studded with shiny pale leaves, adding a spring fever feel.

We were unanimous, voting to stop for lunch in this charming place. Mike, our driver, agreed.

Not too surprisingly, the word soon got around town that a busload of hunky men had invaded France and were chowing down downtown. Can't imagine why. Seventeen tall Chips in muscle shirts, tank tops, and jeans drinking beer and laughing was enough to entice even Tinkerbell out of the castle for a look-see.

Someone had ratted that we were the Chippendales on the way to Paris. When we finished and headed back to the parking lot a couple of blocks over, we had a following of twenty or so forward females, all begging for autographs.

Suddenly, another thirty swarmed around us like bears after honey.

As I signed my autograph for a cute teenager, Mike came running toward us from the parking lot behind the block of cafes. "Go back, go back. There's a riot around the bus. Can't get to it."

How much riot could there be?

Mike pushed and shoved us. "Back to the cafe."

The crowd surrounding us quickly swelled by a

third as the screeching started. "Chippendales . . . Chippendales." I'd heard that sound before in a peep show place in Antwerp.

Mike yelled again. "Can't make it back. Quick, everybody, in here." He pointed at the open door of a flower shop welcoming spring temperatures, not yelling groupies on the verge of panic.

Mike propelled me inside. The others quickly followed, pulling and shoving away from frantic hands trying to rip our shirts off.

Darrell was the last one in, before Mike shut the door.

Needless to say, two anxious clerks and three female customers were shaken by our sudden salvo. The shopkeeper started yelling in French. I couldn't understand the words, but the message was clear. He wanted us the hell out of his store.

Mike tried to calm him, speaking broken French.

The man retorted loudly in English, "Get out! Get out! You tear the flowers. Step on plants. You pay. You pay!"

Now that we were on the safe side of the door, the whole scene seemed like something out of a Jim Carrey film. Mike arguing with the florist half in French, half in English, while all of us laughed and pointed at faces pressed against the large windowpanes. One aggressive teenager pulled up her blouse and pressed her naked tits against the glass.

The screaming became louder. The girls were pushing at the glass-paneled door, threatening to break it any second.

The florist picked up the phone and dialed. Probably calling the gendarmes. None too soon! We'd need a riot squad to get us out of this place with body parts still attached.

This impromptu rampage was bound to make the local paper. I could see the headline: Chippendales Find Little Shop of Horrors in Lille Florist Shop.

Darrell, standing next to me laughing, stopped and shouted, "Hey, Mike . . . Mike? Ask him if there is a way out back."

After checking the rear door and alleyway, Mike yelled at us and pointed. "We can sneak out. . . . No. Wait. They'll still be all around the bus. Better wait for a police escort."

No doubt about it, we were under siege. A Normandy invasion in reverse. Half the guys were now making obscene gestures at the girls out front and teasing them by pulling up their tank tops and flexing their muscles. A couple even unzipped to show their well-filled thongs.

Larry was shouting, "Someone turn on some music. Let's give 'em a show."

More laughter. The Chips were loving every minute of it.

No one seemed concerned with angry mob rule, no one except me. I'd had my own life-threatening experience on stage, thank you very much.

Just as some of the girls pushed the front runners forward, the door glass broke inward.

Blood sprinkled the resulting shards. A couple of the girls had been cut. The screams closest to us took on a hysterical tone. Those behind the injured girls pressed on, ever intent on tearing cloth souvenirs off us.

The peculiar seesaw wailing sounds heading our way made me think of the Pink Panther movies. The cavalry was on the way again, this time in the form of Lille gendarmerie.

Apparently, the mob of girls heard the sirens, too. Some of them backed off, helping the injured girls away from the broken glass door.

A few minutes later, enough whistles to referee the Super Bowl game were blowing out front. French gendarmes were swinging clubs threateningly. Not hitting anyone, not yet, anyway.

It was a mean bunch of groupies out there, switching fickle, pent-up wrath onto the authorities.

The guys around me stopped laughing. Shirts down and zippers up.

I was a bit paranoid; I'd listened to Mark and hadn't brought any pot, thinking the border guards would run us all into the slammer with little provocation. I knew Cody had something in his pocket now. He'd placed I-don't-know-what in a plastic bag and shoved it up his asshole before crossing the border. Taking chances was penny-ante poker to him.

What if the gendarmes searched him? Not a pretty picture.

I could hear Mark Pakin cursing all the way from Brussels.

It took a good thirty minutes for the troops to disperse the crowd enough to escort us to the bus. They hadn't searched anyone, thank the Lord.

Before Mike could get the bus moving, we were surrounded again by screaming piranha. They were new fish, apparently having gotten the word of our arrival late.

Several women were ripping their tops off. The bus couldn't leave now because yelling girls had surrounded it. Some even climbed up the back ladder and ran overhead along the top. They were all demanding we get out. They left little doubt what they were after. God, if Lille was like this, what was waiting for us in Paris?

We were snapping pictures of the girls. One finally stood in front of the bus and removed her T-shirt, jeans, and panties. She pranced back and forth, ample tits bouncing like Club Copa strippers.

The gendarmerie were back to our rescue again, cursing the women with one breath, us with the next.

Finally, they cleared a path by backing a police car up to the front of our bus. This was a clear signal to pull away and follow the escort out of town.

As we reached the outskirts of Lille unscathed, Mike announced on the speaker that the police had told him in no uncertain terms to get us out of town and "don't come back." Sort of like Eliot Ness threatening Al Capone. They had better things to do than play nurse-maid to a bunch of nudist sickos.

Nudist sickos? Now we were nudist sickos? Mark Pakin had been right. The French men might not like Americans, but the women sure did.

We arrived mid-afternoon in Paris and checked into a small hotel on the Left Bank of the Seine River. Because Mark Pakin wasn't paying for our stay, we'd agreed on less expensive digs for the night following the show.

Just think of it. I was in Paris, France. Romantic capital of the world. The Louvre, the Champs Elysées, Notre Dame, the Bastille, Latin Quarter, none of which I'd have the chance to see.

We only had time for a quick dinner before heading to the Palais des Congres Theater. Above the marquee out front was a twenty-foot banner, a blow-up of our famous Chippendale poster highlighted with spotlights.

We'd been warned by Mark to arrive and enter the theater just before the opening number and sit in the last row on the first floor reserved for us. The idea for the back seats was the ability to get in and out easily without creating havoc and screwing up Number Two's show. We'd had enough riot for one day.

Since the French women were on their feet so much

of the time, we constantly had to stand to see the performance. The Chips in the show were good, but, in my humble opinion, not on a par with our cast. All of us were whispering about different movement styles of the dancers, toned-up lighting, overly loud sound effects, everything in general.

The research bit was working for me. I picked up a couple of tips on presenting my solo numbers on stage. For one thing, the lead singer for the Paris show was more graceful with his hands. He also moved more lightly about the stage. Much better dancer than I, but who wasn't?

The performance was okay until the "Cream" number, the one featuring the top banana. An African-American Chip listed as Travis led the safari for one. It was obvious why he had been chosen for the part. He was amply endowed, stretching his thong to an un-Tarzan-like limit.

At the end of the number, he slowly pulled the thong off, back to the audience. This was where the number in our show blacked out.

Not in Paris! The music continued another chorus while the black dude spread his legs to the beat, still stomping his feet. You've got to be kidding! Even from the back of the house I could see his dick hanging almost to his knees, jumping back and forth like Jack's beanstalk on the rise.

That's not in the rule book. The spotlight was supposed to be no lower than his cheeks.

Guess Parisians expected more. They certainly got it with Travis. John Holmes, take a hike!

I'm serious; it was so long that, when he swung it like a limp rope, propeller-like, back still to the audience, I could see the head extending beyond his ass cheeks on each side.

I couldn't imagine anyone being attracted to anything so gargantuan. The ladies in the crowd obviously disagreed with my viewpoint as they yelled, laughed, and pointed.

After the show, our two groups went out to a club together. The Paris cast was heavy into hard drugs, especially Ecstasy. Everybody was quickly stoned or drunk or both. Drugs, booze, and women — that's all we talked about, that and Travis and his super dog, Wonder!

I met Travis's current girlfriend, a petite, white, French girl, later that night in his hotel room where we shared grass. How was she able to accommodate Travis's male marvel? Don't ask.

19

The end of the second week of May, I called home to let my parents know I was still alive. By now, they were resigned to my new show business career. They even asked me to send them a Chippendale show program. Their most interesting news was about the invitation to my Wenatchee High School ten-year reunion to be held the fourth week of May at the local convention center.

What I wouldn't do to be there. Bragging rights about the tour and my budding film career would be just the beginning. And I'd be home to see Rene. I missed her so much.

However, I had another five shows to do before our break. I'd miss the reunion. We were to have six weeks off before starting a second five-and-a-half-month tour in Europe the middle of July.

Wait a minute! What if I could get Mark Pakin to

let me skip the last two shows. I could make the re-union with a couple of days to spare.

What the hell! It was worth a try.

Suffice it to say, Mark was not pleased with my request.

"Look, Troy, you haven't exactly been cooperative the past couple of months. I've constantly asked you to work into more of the dancing numbers. You haven't even tried. What's more, you've broken about every rule in the book, including walking out on one of my meetings. Give me one reason why I should let you cut the last two shows."

"I know," I said. "I haven't done everything I should. I've been in the doldrums lately. Don't like myself very much. I need to work things out in my mind." My bouts of feeling low lately were really getting to me. It was vital I get a rest, a rest back home. I just needed to get away from this crazy scene for awhile.

Mark looked at me hard. "And why doesn't that surprise me? You guys are all alike. You dope up and drink yourselves into oblivion, screw all night, then wonder what's going wrong. Get real! You've gotten yourself into this mess, not me. Don't try to blame anyone but yourself. Face up to the problem and do something about it."

If one of the guys had talked to me about this shit, maybe I would have paid attention. Coming from the boss, however, it was just bullshit.

"You're right, Mark." If I wanted to, I could be political with the best of them.

I tried another tactic. "The ladies won't miss me for just a couple of shows. Bob can fill in. He knows my part backward and forward." Bob, an Arizonan from Phoenix, was also one of the new guys on the beat, fairly good singer, and he danced better than I did. I wasn't about to mention that part.

Mark looked at me and sighed. "Okay. You can go. But you'd better come back with a changed attitude. Got it?"

"Yeah. You're on."

Mark even arranged and paid for my ticket back home from Dusseldorf, Germany.

As for me? I still had problems. I'd tried to find euphoria through negatives foreign to my system, but it didn't seem to work. Maybe I was just homesick.

I let my parents know when to expect me, then called my daughter with the good news.

That night in Brussels, following our last Theater 140 show engagement, attractive twin 20-year-old Belgian girls in identical print minidresses started hitting on me at the Mirano Continental, my favorite disco club in the city.

One twinky twin was enough. What was I going to do with two? Get another Chip, of course. The girls didn't want to come to my room without another guy. Cindy and Nanette were inseparable.

Because Brent had an overnight date with a guy in

Brussels, I had the hotel room to myself. I didn't want to waste it.

The other Chippendale guys at Club Mirano were already set with girls, everyone except Cody. He was always so blitzed on drugs that he never wanted to leave. I often wondered what he did when the rest of us were fucking the night away.

"Come on, Cody. It'll be sex with a capital 'S.' The twins are hot for your body, can't you tell?"

I was laying it on thick, desperate not to lose Cindy, or was it Nanette? Didn't seem to matter. Actually, I might have been able to talk them into joining me anyway if I couldn't get Cody to capitulate. "Double your pleasure, double your fun, sleep with two women instead of just one." After all, I'd discovered such diversion on the Viking Cruise ship crossing the Baltic Sea.

"Oh, man. I don't know. I just as soon stay here and disco." His words were already drifting, blurred with coke, I think. I wasn't sure what his drug of choice was that night. Could have been acid.

"Just for a little while. If you don't like it, you can leave."

"Sure?"

"Sure."

Thirty minutes later, we were in my room at the Amigo Hotel.

Cody insisted on drinks all around. I pulled out a bottle of Smirnoff I was saving for Germany, broke the seal, then added tonic to glasses of ice.

The girls took two sips, and started dropping their minidresses. They were naked underneath. I was out of my clothes in a flash.

Cody sat in a chair and watched, taking small sips of his vodka and tonic, ogling us.

I was hot with a woody any tree would be proud of. I no longer felt shy around another guy in a sexual situation. Habits change. Practice eliminates inhibitions.

I got into bed on my back and pulled Cindy on top. As we slid around French kissing, with hands searching out private amorous spots, I glanced sideways at Cody, still sitting in the chair, staring. Nanette was pulling at his shirt buttons.

I was more concerned with other pursuits, with Cindy pole-vaulting on top.

I looked over at Cody again. He was naked, sitting in the chair, stroking his erection, ignoring Nancy's manipulations, just watching us.

The next thing I knew, Cody was standing by the bed.

Cindy reached back and started playing with my balls.

It took me a second to realize Cody's hand was rubbing my leg somewhere down there.

Nanette was behind him, reaching around playing with his erection. Whatever!

Suddenly, Cindy pulled off me and started French kissing again. I felt a hand creeping up my leg.

I pulled my lips away from Cindy long enough to see it was Cody, eyes glazed, ignoring Nanette, right hand heading for my dick! "Cody? What are you doin', man?"

Cody kept at it. "What you fuckin' wanted me to do all along, that's all."

My dick wilted like a morning glory at noon. I jerked Cody's hand off my leg and sat up, dumping poor Cindy off the bed. She responded with French cursing.

Cody, in his comatose state, said, "Just having a little extra fun . . . that's all, buddy. Don't mind, do you?"

I shouted, "I sure as hell do!"

I swung my feet onto the floor and pushed Cody away from me.

Damn! This was something I expected from Brent throughout the tour, not one of the straight guys. Then it dawned on me. This must be why Cody never took girls to his room.

Nanette just stood there, cursing us. "You fags? Why you no say so?"

"No. We're not—"

"Come, Cindy. We go." She pulled her minidress over her quivering tits.

I was too stunned by Cody's actions to say anything. I nodded, stared at them, and said lamely, "Sorry, girls. Maybe another time."

They were gone, leaving me with a still amorous-looking Cody. He moved back to me and reached between my legs.

I stiff-armed him away and shouted, "Cody. What the hell! I don't want your hands on me. Don't know why the fuck you thought I was queer." My words were harsher than intended.

"Shit, I'm not . . . either." Cody backed away and flopped into a chair as if suddenly coming to his senses. His sigh sounded painful. "Just wanted to get it on with—"

He lost it, bursting into great, child-like sobs.

Was this sort of a coming-out-of-the-closet kind of thing with Cody?

I wasn't about to get near him even for a much-needed cigarette.

I sat there while he sobbed. Was his performance drug-drenching? No. Gut-wrenching.

Still naked, I felt vulnerable. I slipped on my jeans and sat on the edge of the bed, waiting for his storm to end.

Finally the sobs lessened, then became sniffles. "I'm sorry, man. I'm stoned. Just couldn't help my—" He started crying again.

I'd never heard anything so pathetic in my life. He was suddenly sober, tearing himself apart. I thought of Brent's confession the night we gave up cigarettes, the obstacles involved in coming out as a homosexual when he was young, much younger than Cody. I think I was witnessing some of the same reactions.

I didn't know what to say, how to stop the flow. I just wanted to get the hell out and away, but it was my room.

I knew leaving him in that state wasn't the right thing to do. I felt some sort of responsibility to a Chippendale, not to blast away at Cody, but to help him talk it out. Hell, I'd become a father confessor the past few months. First Ernie, then Russell, then Brent. Guess one more turn in the confessional booth wouldn't kill me.

I fixed us each another vodka and handed a glass to Cody. He was now morose, staring at the flowered wallpaper as if new foliage would start sprouting any minute. He'd pulled on his Chip black pants and T-shirt.

In as calm a voice as I could muster, given the situation, I said, "You want to talk about it?"

He looked up, put the drink down on a side table without taking a sip, then shook his head. "No. I can't."

"Suit yourself, man. I was just trying to help."

"Really?"

"Yeah."

"No one can help." He shook his head again, hang-dog.

"Okay. Let's go back to the club and—"

"If I do, you have to promise not to tell anyone, Troy. Not anyone. Ever." He still couldn't look at me.

I shook my head. "Don't worry. I won't." Seemed like I'd used that phrase before. "Talk to me if you want to or don't. I won't say anything to anyone about it. Promise."

Cody straightened, then looked at me for the longest time. He sighed. "I've had these feelings awhile now. About men, I mean. Couldn't talk to anyone about it. Not even the gay guys in the cast. You probably noticed I never take a woman back to my hotel room."

I sat on the edge of the bed, watching his eyes. "I noticed. Listen, Cody, Brent's the one you need to talk to. He's a great guy, and he'll understand the feelings. I don't. Not the way he will. He's been all through this sort of shit."

Cody shook his head. "No. I don't know if I can get up the courage to say this again to anyone." He was still looking at the wall. "Haven't had sex with a girl since high school. Don't think I could get it up with one. But seeing you and—"

His expression was filled with anguish. "I've never let myself do anything like this before." His voice trailed off. He started again, voice a whisper. "I dream of doing it all the time, touching a man, feeling him up. It's never a woman in my dreams . . . just a good-looking guy . . . like you."

I didn't know whether to be flattered or offended.

"Fantasies. Always fantasies. I'm sorry I touched you, Troy. It wasn't right. Fuck! I didn't even ask. I just couldn't . . . help myself. All the coke and pent-up feelings were just too much. Please forgive me, Troy."

It was my turn to sigh. "Nothing to forgive. It's all

right, Cody. No damage done. Probably some good will come out of your . . . talking about it though. Maybe now you can let yourself be who you really want to be. Need to be. Let yourself search out guys who feel the same way."

Was this me talking? An Assembly of God refugee who'd been taught homosexuals were two steps below the Antichrist? Who made me Dr. Ruth?

Cody shook his head. "Who am I, Troy?"

I placed my vodka glass on the nightstand. "Hell, Cody, I've been trying to figure that one out about myself for awhile."

He nodded. "With me, it's been going on at least five years. Sad. Fuckin' sad, isn't it?"

I looked at him, then waited until I had his full attention. "Cody, you need to do one thing for me . . . for yourself."

He jerked his head up, a glint of hope in his countenance.

"Have a heart-to-heart with Brent. He'll understand your needs. He'll be discreet. I've gotten to know him pretty well. He's an honest guy. He'll protect your privacy. I know he will."

An expression of relief spread across his face. "You think so?"

"I know so."

His gut-wrenching sigh was enough to bring tears to a grown man's eyes.

Our conversation ended on a pleasant note. Cody

dressed and left, promising to talk to Brent at the first opportunity.

I told Cody I wouldn't say anything to Brent about it. I would not invade his privacy any further than I already had.

I thought about returning to the club. Then my mind started working over the scene I'd just witnessed.

What the hell! All God's creatures gotta do their thing. Cody included.

20

Northeast of Brussels, equidistant from Amsterdam, lies Dusseldorf, a glittering showcase for all the good things the deutschemark can buy. Germany's fashion capital at the confluence of the rivers Rhine and Dussel is a rich city endowed with German new money. Though Dusseldorf, meaning "Village on the Dussel" was almost completely destroyed in World War II, it is today a metropolis of new buildings, richness of culture, and thriving business.

We arrived early afternoon at the Hotel Esplanade, a modern building similar to an American Holiday Inn.

I was anxious to get back home, not only for my high school reunion, but to see Rene. I wasn't being much of a father thousands of miles away. Besides, I was burned out, ready for the promised six weeks off. Though candles burn at both ends, mine had flickered out in the extremities.

The second night of *Chippendales: The Scandinavian Tour*, Ernie, in front of our jean curtain, gave me a testimonial halfway through the second act about going to Hollywood and appearing in *Dutch Treat*. He hyped me more than I expected, laying it on thick. I suspected it was a sort of disclaimer that we weren't just a bunch of stupid strippers, but had potential in the real show business world. Sounded good to me.

The curtain was to rise to show a Chip waiter, wearing our signature bow tie, cuffs, and tight pants, standing by a small dining table set for a candlelit dinner for two.

Another Chip would pick out a pleasingly plump young lady from the audience and bring her on stage for a make-believe dinner. The Chip waiter, Cody, would lip-sync my recorded number as the other Chip poured wine, etc.

That night, because I'd always wanted to wear the Chip costume and was leaving the show temporarily, I talked Cody into letting me be the waiter. I was soon lip-syncing my own recording.

Ernie picked up on the switch immediately. "And here is our Hollywood-bound boy now, Troy."

To the pretty, shy girl now sitting at the table center stage, the switch made no difference.

I surprised even myself as I got into the number, a good deal more clumsily than Cody, and started the strip. All I had to take off was his apron, boots, and stretch pants with Velcro strips on the sides. I wore only the collar, bow tie, and cuffs above the waist. By the end of the second chorus, I was all the way down to my thong bikini. It was the first time I'd worn one. I felt totally naked in the spotlight even with this slip of cloth over the important parts.

Somehow, I made it through, with Ernie looking at me from the wings, chuckling all the while. I continued to the part where I was supposed to lift the girl's hand to my crotch. This is where the blackout always occurred, with her hand never reaching me.

No blackout! What?

I looked backstage frantically. I wanted to shout, "Somebody cut the damn lights."

Obviously someone, probably Ernie, had encouraged the guys backstage to start the recording again at the beginning of the second chorus.

No! You sons of bitches! Of course, I couldn't say anything. What to do? Start lip-syncing again.

I placed the girl's hand gently onto the table. She was well into the scene now and wasn't about to let a good feel escape her big night on stage. She yanked her hand right back, all the way onto my crotch this time, and squeezed.

The guys in the wings were in hysterics.

I stepped back suddenly enough to pull the young woman out of the chair and sprawling onto the stage.

The laughter from out front was thunderous. She still hadn't let go. One of Cody's Velcro fastenings on the side came apart. Do I fix it, or help the girl up?

It was obvious which choice the audience preferred.

I reached for the girl's hand and helped her stand, still lip-syncing my song, and led her off stage right. As I reached the wings, I unfastened the other side of the thong and let it drop to the stage floor.

The crowd went wild. I don't know what possessed me to finish the non-scripted strip. Been watching too many shows, I guess.

I immediately apologized to the girl, explaining that ending wasn't supposed to happen. It was my last night in the show, and the other Chips had played a prank on me — traditional in the theater on closing nights.

She understood. I got her a copy of my picture from the dressing room and autographed it.

I still laugh at my debut as a Chip dancer, a fitting end to this part of the tour.

After the show that night, I said my goodbyes, taking a lot of ribbing about my big scene. I guess I expected more of a "We'll miss you, guy." No way. "See you soon" was more in order. Only Brent spent a couple of minutes wishing me a good time in Wenatchee. I'm sure he was happy to have a room to himself for the next few days.

I was supposed to leave right away for the Dusseldorf Airport for an all-nighter: KLM Royal Dutch Airlines to Amsterdam, switch planes to New York, then switch again to Northwest Airlines at Kennedy for Sea-Tac in Seattle.

I heard all the guys were going to a nightclub in an area called Altstadt. Because I had a couple of hours to kill before the flight, I decided I'd surprise everyone there. I splurged on a cab to the Metro Club.

I entered the noisy nightclub without an entourage. The place was filled with Germans, laughing, drinking, dancing. The Chips weren't there, not even one. Obviously, they'd switched nightspots.

What was worse, I was completely ignored by the patrons. That was a shocker. I was used to a big entrance with the gang, with all the girls gathering around and fawning all over us.

I didn't know anyone here. No one approached to welcome a Chippendale. The Chips always leaned on one another after hours. There was more power with eight or ten of us.

I felt the insecurity of being alone all the way to my toes. Nothing felt right. For some reason, that fixation clouded my reasoning. My anxiety was more engrossed with flying solo in the real world than about going home. It was as if I was leaving my new life here for a vacation to someplace foreign. I wasn't at all sure I wanted that vacation now.

Everyone spoke German. None of the girls in the Metro paid the slightest attention to me. I'd have to become the aggressor if I wanted to pick up someone. This was a new role for a Chippendale. Pick and choose the girls throwing themselves at you had always been the segue into the wee hours.

It was the first time I realized the sexual power of being a stage personality. Without it, I was just an average guy on the make.

I stood at the bar about thirty minutes, sipping a draft dark beer. A headache began in the back of my skull and crept forward. I was restless, in need of pot. I'd given what I had left to Cody. I hadn't wanted to risk having customs in New York find drugs on me. I couldn't take any more of this "real-life" shit.

I bagged it and took another taxi to the airport, headache throbbing. I'd swallow a couple of Tylenol and zonk out on the airplane.

When I got to the KLM ticket counter at midnight, I discovered my ticket home was for five days later, the date the rest of the company was scheduled to leave Europe. Mark hadn't updated it nor changed my reservation. Fortunately, the space was available.

The female ticket agent spoke accented English. "I'm afraid, sir, it'll cost an additional two hundred U.S. to switch to the flight tonight."

"What? Two hundred? But it was a mistake. My tour manager got the date mixed up, that's all."

"Tour manager?" Her eyes lit up.

I turned on the old Chip charm. "I just finished a tour with the Chippendales and am taking a break before the next tour starts in England."

"Really? I thought I recognized you. You're a . . . of course, you are. I saw you in the show last night. You were one of the singers, weren't you?"

I laughed. "Yep. That was me." I looked down the row of counters. The plain-looking thirtyish ticket agent was twenty feet away from the only other agent this time of night. After all, the start of my air journey was a commuter flight to Amsterdam. "Look, there must be something you can do about the fee, can't you?"

She hesitated.

"What if I gave you a Chippendale calendar?"

She smiled.

"And . . . and threw in a Chip T-shirt? Would that help?"

It was her turn to look down to the next airline counter. She nodded. "Wouldn't hurt."

I rummaged in my carry-on and pulled out the desired items. I'd brought several for gifts back home. I slid them across the counter.

She grabbed them quicker than a panhandler finding a tin can in the garbage.

She altered my ticket and handed me a boarding pass. "Have a nice flight, Mr. Kline."

I smiled back. "Thank you. Too bad you can't join me." I patted her hand.

When I looked back, she was heading through a door, smiling over her ill-gotten gains.

As I headed toward the boarding gate, I thought about the English tour coming up in six weeks. New frontiers to conquer when I returned. New girls. Lots and lots of new girls. I'd be rested, ready and waiting for even greater adventures.

21

I arrived at Seattle-Tacoma Airport at 2:30 on a rainy Tuesday afternoon, May 16, grubby and ready to sack out in a bed. Never could sleep on airplanes.

Kathy, the girlfriend I'd left behind in my quest for immortality, had used my Blazer while I was gone, so from Germany I had arranged with her to meet my flight, a ten-minute drive to Sea-Tac from her apartment in Federal Way.

I planned to stay with Kathy the next three nights, then head over to Wenatchee on Friday. The high school reunion weekend was to start Saturday.

Kathy was at the Northwest Airlines gate, smiling.

I suddenly realized she wasn't the most attractive girl I'd ever dated. Stringy brunette hair, too much makeup, and unattractive teeth. I'd been spoiled by all the natural, beautiful, blonde women in Scandinavia. What did I ever see in Kathy in the first place?

The attraction must have been the free place to store my car while I was gallivanting about Europe.

She chatted all the way to Federal Way, telling me all about her new job as a teller for Seafirst Bank. She sat so close that I had trouble shifting gears.

Later, at her cluttered apartment, she was all over me like cotton candy on a tube. I felt sticky, clammy, claustrophobic, and tired. My headache had returned, and Kathy was boring, still going on about cashier's checks and customers. I'd forgotten how tiresome her conversation could be. Worse than that, she wouldn't let me talk about myself and my adventures. I'd had a hell of an experience in Scandinavia. I wanted to share it with someone. She was the only one around.

After a few mouthfuls of her soggy spaghetti, I crashed, too beat to keep up my side of the conversation.

She slipped into bed, naked. Hell! I must have been tired; I didn't even want to screw. I did anyway, an unenthusiastic, gratuitous fuck to thank her for taking care of the Blazer.

Early the next morning, Wednesday, I was out of there, heading for Wenatchee. No way was I going to spend two days and nights with chatty Kathy. I promised to call her when I got back to Seattle even though I had no intention of doing so.

I'd have to find another home for my Blazer before heading to England.

When I stopped at a Texaco to fill the tank, I called

Mom at work. I'd be in Wenatchee about one o'clock. She was delighted that I'd be there a couple of days early.

Heading down Interstate 90 through Issaquah, I started to drive down Front Street to say hello to my friend and mentor at Hair Company, the beauty salon I'd worked at before heading overseas. I decided I didn't have time. I wanted to spend more than a few minutes with James. Plenty of time when I came back from Wenatchee. I knew I wouldn't be able to take more than a few days at home.

The sunshine brightened my mixed feelings about being back. The drive over Snoqualmie Pass in the Cascade Mountains was magnificent as usual, leaves out on the trees, snow still on the upper slopes — not enough for spring skiing, though. I had no highway problems driving through Cle Elum and taking the Bluett Pass Highway through more Cascade Mountains to Wenatchee. I made it home in record time.

Though it was good to see my parents that evening, we didn't have a lot to talk about other than the scenery and the sightseeing I'd done while on tour. I could hardly tell them about the show scenes or the after-hours antics. I cut my initial visit short to drive over to Linda's house to see my five-year-old daughter, Rene.

I hugged her as though I'd squeeze all the breath out of her. I'd brought her back a teddy bear wearing a Tyrolean hat and lederhosen I'd picked up at the Dusseldorf Airport. Typical dad, forgetting to buy something special for his daughter before arriving home.

Rene loved it.

Linda seemed happy to see me, too. Her boyfriend had moved in with her a few months back. He was congenial. We liked each other from the start. It was obvious he was good to them. That helped me through the anxious part, having someone kind taking care of Rene, unlike Linda's previous woman-beating bastard.

Rene and I chatted straight for two hours until it was her bedtime. I read her a story and kissed her good night, tears welling in my eyes. She was so sweet and innocent. Guilt crept in. If she only knew what I'd been up to the past five months.

It would be hard to leave her again for Europe. At least I'd spend as much time with her as possible while I was home.

When I got back to my parents' house, Dad was already in bed. Mom had waited up to talk.

When she asked if I had gotten lonely way over there in those foreign ports, I told her about my day in Oslo in Stortorget Square smelling the flowers.

During the next two days at home, to their credit, my parents didn't once mention when I was coming back to Washington to stay. That was cool. We seemed to get along better than we ever had when I was growing up.

Even cooler, my Mom asked for a Chippendale calendar. I'd given one to Kathy and was saving the last one for Joanie, my best female friend in Seattle. I told Mom that I'd send her one from Europe.

I brought Rene over to stay with us the next day and night. It was great being with her again. On Friday, she and I made a trip over to Leavenworth, a replica of a German town at the foot of the Cascade Mountains, thirty miles west of Wenatchee. The town was bursting with tourists shopping for trinkets they didn't need.

The sunshine brightened all the buildings dripping with gingerbread trim, making them shiny and new-looking. A riot of lobelia, petunias, and geraniums bloomed in hanging baskets, trailing from every lamppost in the small tourist area downtown. A German polka band played in the town square.

I explained to Rene that I'd seen buildings like these in Germany. I bought her a nice Sunday dress in one of the better apparel shops.

Not surprisingly, my father didn't say a whole lot to me during my Wenatchee stay. He'd just settle in front of the family room TV following dinner to watch the news and his favorite sitcoms. So what else was new? He wasn't particularly interested in my European tour. But then, he'd never been particularly interested in my pursuits even as a kid. Why should he be any different now?

Linda agreed to go with me to the ten-year high school reunion at the Wenatchee Convention Center.

The main hall that night was decorated with endless

loops of purple and gold crepe paper. School banners showing a leaping panther were pinned to each end of a stage-wide purple and gold banner proclaiming "WELCOME CLASS OF '83." It had been ten long years since our 300 or so class members graduated.

"Linda and Troy Kline," a wide-eyed Marsha greeted us. "I don't believe it. You look wonderful. How are you?"

"Great." Linda looked at me. Of course, many of those here wouldn't know we were no longer married. We'd cross the divorce bridge as we came to it.

I paid for our tickets, then paused as Marsha pinned buttons the size of Mason jar lids onto my sport coat and Linda's blue sequined party dress. Yearbook pictures had been transferred onto them.

Linda looked at my picture and laughed. "We didn't actually look this geeky, did we?"

"Afraid so."

I quickly joined the crowd around the bar.

It took only a couple of guys asking me what I was doing now before the news flashed around the 250 or so attendees like a whisper campaign. "Troy's a Chippendale. A what? A Chippendale. You know the male strippers in those clubs where women stick money in their G-strings. No shit? You're kidding. No. He said so himself."

By the time Linda and I were into our second drink, the girls were sticking around me like flies to a bug zapper and just as sizzling. Girls I never had a chance with in high school were falling all over themselves to be close.

The remarkable thing about the old crowd was that no one seemed to have changed. They were still doing the same old thing. A third of them still lived in Wenatchee, where there was no other choice but the same old thing.

The conversation was not stimulating. I tried hard not to brag about my experiences in Europe. That was a switch for me. All along, I'd planned to regale listeners with details of the tour, especially getting into the nitty-gritty with the guys. Somehow, it didn't seem appropriate. I was back on my old stomping grounds, drowning in old habits and old conversations, with old religious hang-ups taunting me at every turn.

I ended up talking about the same topics I'd discussed with my parents, the great cities I'd visited. However, I did describe my part in the show scenes.

I didn't belong to this old life any more than I belonged to the new one as a Chippendale. Cody had asked it correctly in Brussels that night of revelation. "Who am I, Troy?" I'd been asking myself that question over and over flying across the Atlantic. Confused was who I was. Mr. Confused-as-hell!

I realized then that I'd come back to the Northwest with a lot of old baggage — the superiority attitudes perfected as a Chippendale. I was too good for these yokels.

I felt embarrassed as harsh reality set in. Back in

Europe, everywhere I went as a Chip, girls wanted my body and my picture. Here, the questions were posed as if I was some kind of freak who got his rocks off removing his clothes. One girl even asked me how many porno films I'd made.

The guys held back their laughter until they were out of my earshot.

My fall from grace into shit was the generally accepted view by one and all. That pissed me off to no end.

None of them understood what kind of show this was. They didn't want to, and I didn't feel like explaining the details to them.

I was trying to make myself out to be a normal schmuck. I was hardly normal. I was a messed-up schmuck having second thoughts about the life I'd been leading and where it was heading.

I was a lost soul, suddenly in a funk with all my high school friends crowding around, pumping me for info about the Chips. A shroud of religious teachings wrapped itself around me, holding on for dear life, even as European funk clung like a wetsuit.

The buffet was lavish for Wenatchee. The local girls and guys had prepared most of it: barbecue ribs, chicken, vegetables, rice, the usual hometown fare they were all accustomed to in Wenatchee. Fare filled with calories. Our show chef, Bill, would have had apoplexy over the menu.

Afterward, between swilling drinks, everybody

danced. I joined the other guys, getting smashed on vodka tonic, while recordings of Michael Jackson, Duran Duran, and Flock of Seagulls blasted away.

Everyone had a good time. The non-drinkers left early. The rest of us recalled old high school stories and pranks, remembering them to be far more daring and fun than they actually were. I began to feel a little better. Though the language and stories got progressively more gross, I still didn't talk about sleeping my way through the girls of Scandinavia. The guys wouldn't have believed those wild stories anyway. I wasn't sure I did.

Linda and I helped close the place down at one a.m. Literally. We helped remove the paraphernalia of which youthful dreams are built. The banner would be used again at the next day's family picnic at Rocky Reach Dam Park.

Throughout the entire evening, I never saw anyone taking drugs. Not one even smoked marijuana. I guess they didn't need it to have a fun time.

I spent the next day drinking beer and eating hot dogs and hamburgers, and talking to my best friend from high school, Kurt. He'd been on the track team with me. Much shorter and slender as a bean on a good day, he had been a faster runner. He'd filled out, now, no longer jogging to keep in shape. His mustache made him look older than 29. His brown eyes were piercing, though. I didn't remember them being so piercing before.

Kurt still lived in Seattle and was still involved with Pursuit of Excellence.

I opened up a little to Kurt, telling him what I'd kept quiet the night before, all about the drugs and sex, about my going off the deep end.

Though he must have been shocked, his reaction didn't give away his feelings. Must have been the training he'd absorbed with Pursuit of Excellence.

I promised to look him up for a beer or two when I got back to Seattle.

I don't know how I survived those two days traveling down memory lane. I didn't actually remember them as being "good old days," just days to endure until Linda and I could board the first stage out of town.

I became convinced that nostalgia should be relegated to scrapbooks stored in an attic trunk.

22

When I returned to Seattle late Monday afternoon following the Wenatchee wear-down, I drove over to Joanie's apartment in Bellevue. She was a practicing nurse now, still at work at Overlake Hospital.

I'd written to Joanie only once during the tour, just to keep in touch with my soulmate. I'd done one better by calling her from Amsterdam about my return to see Rene and attend the Wenatchee High School reunion. She invited me to stay with her while I was in Seattle before heading back on tour. "What are friends for?" was her straightforward comment.

Her candor touched me.

During the day in Europe, when I wasn't stoned or drunk, I'd often contemplated the possibility of our friendship becoming more.

Her welcome that Monday evening after the Wenatchee reunion seemed genuine and heartfelt. I know mine was. We opened a bottle of Chenin Blanc, sat on the couch, and I told her all about my show. She was the first person truly interested in the minute details of my Scandinavian adventures.

She encouraged me to describe every number in the show, each moment, how the audience reacted, asking me to zoom in on my specific scenes. I told her all the funny details of opening night, the soap problem in the shower, the baked bean scene, the Harley accident, my being attacked on stage, and the impromptu strip my last night in Dusseldorf.

We laughed the evening away about all the Chippendale antics while we finished one bottle of Chenin Blanc and started on another.

I stopped short of telling her about the orgies and drugs, but described the beauty of Norway, taking her along all the tour cities like a video travelogue, talking about the picketing in Helsinki and the riot in Lille.

We talked and giggled until three in the morning, then fell into bed naked, having sex in a familiar way, nothing kinky. I felt her love for me. I gave mine to her. A sexual love is like no other.

Though we didn't have intercourse again while I stayed with her, we catapulted our friendship to a new level, one without need for physical gratification.

I spent time with my mentor, James, and revisited Cafe DaVinci's. The six weeks flew by like Seattle summers. Any day now, I'd be returning to pride and glory in England for God and country.

At the end of June, while still staying with Joanie in Seattle, I called Mark Pakin in Santa Monica to arrange for my return ticket to Europe and the second part of the tour. I was looking forward to experiencing London, Big Ben, Trafalgar Square, Piccadilly Circus, the West End theater district, and all the tradition of royalty. Though I had mixed feelings about returning to that destructive lifestyle, I was still young and full of longing for same.

"Hi, Mark. This is Troy Kline in Seattle. How's it going?"

"Oh, hello, Troy. Busy, busy. Trying to get everything arranged for London. You have a good rest?"

"Yeah. Great. Raring to go." I related my incident with KLM in Dusseldorf. He apologized for not having straightened out the reservation. "How about the ticket to London? Do I pick it up somewhere in Seattle, or are you going to mail it to me?"

Mark hesitated. "Glad you called, Troy. I didn't know how to reach you." His second hesitation sounded ominous. "I'm afraid Chippendales won't be needing you for the rest of the tour."

I felt my heart beat speed up. Did I hear him right? "What do you mean, you won't be—"

"I'm sorry things didn't work out with you, Troy. You have a beautiful voice, but frankly, you're just too much trouble. Your attitudes were not what they should have been. You didn't put your all into the show."

I was flabbergasted. "You can't be serious, Mark?"

"Afraid so. I've already found a replacement. His voice is as good as yours, and he dances beautifully. And he doesn't have an attitude. He'll be better for the show. And that's what counts . . . the show. I always have to look out for what's best for the production. That's my job."

I almost dropped the phone receiver. How could this be? One minute I was heading to London, the next I was buried in Seattle. Even though I had broken every rule in the Chippendale contract twice over, I thought I was indispensable to the show. Not so! No one is indispensable to the show. Well, maybe the star. I wasn't the star. I'd just been told I was actually a detriment to the production.

"But, Mark, I didn't know you felt this way. Why didn't you tell me in Europe? I wouldn't have left early."

"I hadn't decided at the time. Your request to leave abruptly sort of put the cap on all the grief you've caused me. Showed your true colors. Your lack of concern for anybody but yourself. I need men that give their all. You never did."

I felt the heat rising to my cheeks. My spine was tingling. "Mark, I can change. I can—"

"Sorry, Troy. I'm afraid it's too late for change, no matter how dramatic. As I said, I've already hired your replacement. He's been rehearsing here in Santa Monica for the past two weeks.

"Look, I've got to go. It's been nice knowing you, Troy. Good luck with your movie. You'll see this is a good move for you in the long run."

"But, Mark . . . I don't know what—"

"Take care, Troy."

The connection was broken.

I sat there in Joanie's apartment still holding the phone receiver, thoughts slamming through my feeble brain. But what about the short run? I'd just been fired. The shock and hurt were catastrophic. The rejection knocked me in the chest like a Tyson stomach punch, a guilt-a-gram taking my breath away.

I dropped the phone receiver into its cradle, then sank into Joanie's couch. My mind whirled. Hell, the other Chips hadn't supported me like they should. Had they known I was going to get canned and hadn't told me? My voice was terrific. I did the show to perfection, well, maybe not total perfection. My nightly romps on the wild side probably did affect my stage performance on occasion. But I was effective in the show. I got a lot of applause after my big number, "The End of the Road," every time. I received repeated requests for autographs in the theater lobbies even though I wasn't a lead.

I had known Mark was sick of me and my depression and my fits of crying and leaning on him at the end of the tour. I didn't realize he wasn't happy with my performances either. He'd wanted me to dance more, take a more active part in the show. I hadn't even tried. But I never dreamed in my wildest imagination he'd actually let me go for not doing so.

Mark's words when I asked him to let me leave a couple of performances early came back to haunt me. "Look, Troy, you haven't exactly been cooperative the past couple of months. I've constantly asked you to work into more of the dancing numbers. You haven't even tried. What's more, you've broken about every rule in the book, including walking out on one of my meetings. Give me one reason why I should let you cut the last two shows."

"I know, I haven't done everything I should. I've been in the doldrums lately. Don't like myself very much. I need to work things out in my mind. . . ."

"And why doesn't that surprise me? You guys are all alike. You dope up and drink yourselves into oblivion, screw all night, then wonder what's going wrong. Get real! You've gotten yourself into this mess . . . not me. Don't try to blame anyone but yourself."

His words of doom had foreshadowed what was to come. I had just been too stupid to realize it and do something about it. Why the hell had I insisted on coming to the dumb reunion anyway? To show off, that's why. And I didn't even do that.

Mark's words continued to ring in my mind, "You've gotten yourself into this mess . . . you've gotten yourself into this mess. You've gotten—"

I fixed myself a vodka and tonic and continued to mull over Mark's words. Hell, other show members have some of the same problems. All of them except Russell booze all night and. . . . No one can live that lifestyle and not have emotional problems: getting stoned and drunk every night and fucking three women a day. How can anyone not? Anyone but Russell! That was food for thought.

But they didn't get fired, did they?

Maybe some of the others got fired, too. I should have asked that question. No. I didn't want to hear the answer if I was the only one. It would have only brought me down more.

I was still trying to blame my being fired on the system, others leading this horse to the drinking trough. What was the other part of that saying? Oh yeah, "But you can't make him drink."

Maybe a little of the blame was settling where it truly belonged. Shit! Mark was right. I had no one else to blame but myself.

Those overwhelming thoughts didn't help matters. I was devastated. If I'd quit, it would have been one thing, but to be blatantly told on the phone that I was history as a Chip? My life had been pillaged!

And what about everybody at home I'd told I was a Chippendale in a big Broadway-type show touring Scandinavia? All my high school reunion friends, parents, my brother and sister, Joanie.

How could I face this embarrassment?

By the time Joanie got home from work that night, I was soused, a tearful drunk, wallowing in self-pity, leaning against the back of the couch, my feet on the coffee table, an empty glass in my hand.

Joanie took one look at me and knew I was not a happy camper. She glanced at the empty vodka bottle on the side table and empty glass clutched in my hand. I didn't even know when I'd run out of liquor.

I couldn't even look at her. "Got fuckin' fired."

Joanie knew I had planned to call Mark Pakin that day.

"What? Who . . . Pakin fired you?"

"Fuckin' fired."

"The bastard! He can't just . . . you have a contract, don't you?"

A glimmer of hope drifted into my consciousness. Hadn't thought about that.

I shook my head slowly. "Doesn't matter worth a shit. I broke every rule in it. Wouldn't stand . . . up in fuckin' court. Joanie . . . I'm a broken Chip." I laughed. "Snapped in two by fate. A broken Chip."

Joanie sat next to me and pulled me into a hug. "Poor guy. What a hellish blow."

If I'd been sober, I'd have been crying on her shoulder. The booze had liberated me somewhat, dulled my senses to the level of not really giving a damn.

I couldn't talk coherently, just kept repeating, "Son of a bitch fired my sorry ass." I laughed again, and slumped back onto the couch.

Joanie removed the vodka bottle and tumbler. "You're drunk, Troy. Sleep it off, then we'll talk. There must be something we can do."

I wasn't so gone as to not catch her pronoun. Good ol' Joanie.

She helped me stagger into the bedroom, where I passed out on the bed fully clothed.

I didn't awaken until eight the next morning. I felt next to me. The sheets were as cold as a hospital bed. No Joanie.

My head was exploding. I felt dizzy and disoriented. What the hell had hit me? I didn't even remember how the previous evening had ended.

I staggered into the bathroom to relieve myself and search the medicine cabinet for Tylenol. I took a couple, then glared at my red eyes in the mirror.

Coffee. Need coffee. Where's Joanie?

Then it hit me between those bloodshot eyes. I had been canned as a Chip yesterday by my boss.

A shiver ran up my spine and collided with my addled brain. I almost dropped the glass of water in the sink.

I headed into the kitchen. Still no Joanie. Then I saw the note magneted to the refrigerator door.

Dear Troy,

> Sorry about what happened to you yesterday. Couldn't stay to talk about it this morning. Had to get to work. Hot coffee is in the thermal pitcher. See you this evening. We'll talk.
>
> Love, Joanie
>
> P. S. Don't do anything stupid!

Despite my pain, I laughed. Don't do anything stupid! I'd already monopolized the word with actions all over Europe. Now it was time to pay the piper.

I sat at the kitchen table, drinking coffee, as my headache began to dissipate.

What was I going to do now? I hadn't planned my life beyond the end of the '93 tour. I'd thought I'd just sign up for another year. That idea was out the chipped window now. All the work, the rehearsals, the performances — out those rose-colored panes.

By the time Joanie got home that June night, my mind was still in a turmoil, but at least I was sober. I hadn't touched a drop all day.

She seemed to appreciate that effort.

We talked and talked and talked. The world was not an oyster, and it wasn't ending, despite how I felt. I still had my voice. I was going to be in a movie coming out in September. I could still cut hair until Hollywood beckoned. I had a lot for which to be thankful.

Bullshit! Though I listened to her analysis of my self-worth, I still couldn't get the jolt of being bounced like a worn-out ball out of my thick skull.

I compared myself and my situation to that of a professional athlete being let go from the team roster. One can't know what it feels like to hear thousands of people shouting your name, adoring you, looking at you like you are some sort of god, unless you've experienced it. You buy into the fantasy. It becomes real.

You begin to cherish the feeling, depend on it. When it's gone, it's like old Seattle burning: everything goes up in flames.

The worse part is the realization that you're not something special at all. You aren't. You're just another fool trying to make a living at doing what you know best.

Though the talks with Joanie helped, my depression started bringing her down with me. I couldn't get over feeling sorry for little Troy Kline.

I didn't have a place to live now. I'd been staying with Joanie, counting the minutes before going back on tour. My money was pretty much shot. I'd used it to pay off bills, all except the $3,000 for the film work in Amsterdam. Still had that in a savings account to continue child support.

I was suddenly without a job, a place to live, or much of a future. I was extremely pessimistic, sullen, and uncommunicative. I had to get on with my life though, somehow.

Joanie didn't have to ask me to leave. I didn't embarrass myself further depending on her hospitality and charity. We were close friends, not a married couple.

Inside of a week, I had rented a room in Issaquah and gotten back my job styling hair at Hair Company.

From that moment on, I floated in a kind of mental chaos, working half-assed during the day and continuing to live the same kind of lifestyle I'd discovered in

Europe — partying, smoking dope, and fucking every girl who was willing.

I was becoming lost again in a drugged haze, escaping from reality and its devastation.

James, my friend and owner of Hair Company, told me repeatedly that I was burning myself to the ground. My ashes would be all that remained of my psyche if I didn't get professional help. That meant a shrink. I shuffled the advice off to Buffalo.

However, I did come to terms with the abrupt end to my Chippendale career. Even though I began to feel Mark's firing me was a blessing from God to get me away from that lifestyle, I continued to live one reminiscent of my fantasy fame. I was partying far too much and screwing around too much. Though I didn't know what I was going to do with my life, it was a strange sort of relief to get back to the real world where the male had to be the aggressor, not the female.

I thought about the Chippendale guys who had been doing the show for a few years. Some of them were really burned out, too. I thought about Ernie and his problems with no home to go to, about Russell and his deceased love, even about Brent and his inability to go back home to unforgiving parents. At least Brent was resigned to and happy with his lot in life.

And what about poor Cody? Did he finally come to terms with his sexuality and come out of that dark closet?

I rationalized that the Chip shot was little more

than a way to get onto life's golf green. It got me into a movie, but not yet into the cup.

My guilt and concern now weren't for being in the show itself, but for my extracurricular activities — the drug environment and casual sex I had developed for selfish amusement without concern for long-term damage or health risks.

Everybody thinks that with fame and money comes happiness. It wasn't that way for me. I knew it before I left Dusseldorf. The lifestyle just brought me down.

Little did I know, I wasn't at the bottom of the tornado funnel yet.

23

In July, I got a call from Brent of all people, all the way from London. He'd called my folks' home, the number I'd left with him, and been given my current one.

"Really tough, Troy," he commiserated after my telling him I'd been fired. "But you're a great singer. You'll make it to the top with the movie."

He filled me in on all the news. Everyone had returned to London except me.

"You'll be happy to know Cody talked to me about . . . you know. Thanks for being so frank with him. You have no idea how much you helped the poor guy out. You literally saved his life, Troy. I'll be forever grateful."

Despite myself, I smiled. At least I'd done someone some good.

Brent said, "We're roommates now in London and

on the rest of the tour. Isn't that a gas? We're pretty involved with each other. He may be Mr. Right for me."

He cleared his throat. "That's why I'm so grateful for what you did."

Wow! My eyes got blurry. "Good for you. For both of you. You'll be good for him. He's a troubled guy." I said the words as if I wasn't.

Brent spoke quietly. "He isn't any more. He's stopped with the drugs. You wouldn't recognize him sober."

I laughed sort of sick-sweetly. "No, I guess I wouldn't."

I sighed. "Wonderful, Brent. I'm glad. You're a super guy and I'm happy for you . . . the two of you."

After a few more minutes of gossip, we promised to keep in touch and hung up. I knew we wouldn't. So did he.

I really felt good about that phone call. It was the best thing that had happened to me in months. At least someone on tour was concerned over my demise.

The euphoria didn't last long.

In August of 1993, urged by James, my Issaquah mentor, I got in touch with Sarah Prentice, the film producer who discovered me in Amsterdam.

"Miss Prentice, this is Troy Kline calling from Seattle."

"Troy who?"

"I'm the Chippendale singer you hired in Amsterdam to do a scene in a film you were producing."

"Oh yes. That Troy Kline. How are you, Mr. Kline?"

"Fine. I don't want to bother you, but I just wondered when *Dutch Treat* is going to be released to the theaters?"

"*Dutch Treat*? Oh. You mean our Lance Billings film."

"Yes that's the one."

"You haven't heard?"

"No. That's why I'm calling."

"I mean about Lance Billings."

"What about him?"

"He died after a dirt bike accident back in May. Was in a coma for two weeks. Sad. Very sad. So young and vibrant. Good actor, too. I had great plans for him. It's heartbreaking when someone so young dies without reaching his dreams."

The words hit home. "Sorry to hear that. I must have still been in Europe when it happened. I hate to sound callous, but that scene at the Club Cellar in Amsterdam was my introduction into the movies. Will the film be out in September, like you said?"

"Oh no. I'm sorry, Mr. Kline. The film was shelved. We'd only completed about a third of it, and with the star killed, we decided to forget the project. Like pouring money down a drain."

Oh no! Shelved? Film shelved? "What does that mean, Miss Prentice?"

"Sorry. It means just what I said. The project is dead. The film will never be produced. I've moved on to another venture."

I felt my voice lower to a whisper. The slats had been knocked out from under me again. One last hope. "Is there a chance you could use me in another of your ventures?"

"There is always a possibility for fresh young acting talent. Why don't you send me your résumé and a picture. Perhaps I can find something."

"I'm a singer, not an actor."

"Oh. A singer. Well, of course, singing parts are very limited in today's marketplace, unless you are well-known.

"I'm sorry, but my other line is waiting. My secretary will give you my current address and you can—"

I thought quickly. "Is there a possibility of getting a copy of my part in the movie . . . you know, so I can add it to my résumé?"

"I'll see what I can do, but don't hold your breath. I'll have your mailing address when you send in your résumé. Good luck, Mr. Clone. Just hold on for my secretary."

Click.

Wonderful! Now I was Mr. Clone without a future in films.

At the end of 1994, I was still working at Hair Company, but my heart wasn't in hair styling. One night, I saw a very attractive girl around my age at my new favorite watering hole and karaoke bar in Seattle, Hunan Harbor. She was with an average-looking guy. Funny how I still compared all young men against Chippendales as if Chips were on some kind of pedestal. When he left for the john, I made a move on her.

I danced with Cheryl on the postage-stamp-sized dance floor to a rock number. Before her boyfriend came back, I'd asked her out to dinner that weekend. "Sorry, thanks, but I'm involved." She wanted to keep it that way. I could see in her eyes, though, that she was interested in me. She watched me intently the whole time I was singing a couple of karaoke numbers.

Six months later, I saw Cheryl again at Hunan Harbor. She was with a girlfriend that night. After reintroducing myself, I asked her out again. She rejected me for the second time.

She wasn't playing hard to get; she was living with a guy, the same guy I'd seen her with six months earlier.

The third time is the charm they say, and it happened at the same bar three weeks later. She gave me her number. From the very first date, we both knew we were going to be together. I fell in love with her very fast.

I replaced her previous boyfriend and moved into her apartment a month after we started dating. We were soon talking about getting married and having children.

Cheryl was the exact opposite of Joanie. She didn't

mince words. She was very sure of herself and her beauty. I appreciated her best when she was naked. She had these perfect breasts, my fantasy kind. Cheryl's worst fault (as if I didn't have any) was jealousy over my relationship with Joanie. She didn't like it one bit. I was still seeing my good friend occasionally after work for a drink, though we only had a platonic friendship. Cheryl couldn't accept our closeness.

Throughout my time with Cheryl, my down-time continued to hang on like a cumulus cloud, threatening to spill dampness over everyone around me, Cheryl in particular.

I was restless and often unable to sleep at night. I felt fatigued and lethargic most of the time. It was hard to get out of bed in the morning. Feelings of "why should I get up?" hung on like a shroud. "I have nothing to do but cut some bitch's hair. What's the use?"

My interest in sex with Cheryl declined, as well as my interest in reading, which had always been an enjoyable pastime. Now I found I couldn't concentrate long enough to finish a chapter in a novel.

At that point, I was smoking pot all the time. Cheryl hated that. I'd try to hide it from her, sneaking tokes when she wasn't around, or go out to a bar after work and invariably come home stoned. The grass was always greener on the other side, off with bar buddies, away from a nagging Cheryl. I didn't realize what I was doing to our relationship. The story of my stoned life!

My financial status was the pits because I hadn't developed a clientele at the hair salon. I wasn't very nice to my customers — mostly sullen, unsmiling, uninterested in chatting with them to gain their confidence. You don't develop a clientele with a sullen and non-caring attitude. You have to schmooze and take extra time with customers, fawning over them. Shit! I wasn't in the mood for all that schmoozing. If they didn't like it, they could go somewhere else. They did!

James was well aware I was heading into the dumpster, just waiting for the garbage detail to pick me up one day. I couldn't see what was happening, or if I did, I didn't care. James kept advising me to seek the help of a psychologist to pull all that acrimony out of my veins.

Because I couldn't sleep at night, I didn't want to constantly awaken Cheryl with my tossing and turning. Therefore, I slept on the couch in the living room of her apartment. It was as much an excuse to smoke pot undisturbed as any other.

After six months living together, Cheryl was fed up. She didn't need this shit. Things were beginning to fail, sexually. We had nothing to fall back on. Our affair had happened too fast. We hadn't built a friendship like the one I had with Joanie. There was nothing left to our relationship. The thought of staying together through thick and thin was the only Band-Aid holding my body together.

The final curtain happened when I came home

again one midnight, wasted. I'd been over at a musician buddy's apartment, singing and smoking dope. Cheryl was waiting for me in the living room with steam coming out of her ears.

"Where the hell have you been? We were supposed to go over to Tony and Mary's for dinner."

I was totally surprised. "No shit. Was that tonight? I thought it was tomorrow night." In truth I'd forgotten all about it. A lot of "forgetting about it" was going on lately. I staggered past her into the bathroom.

She was still fuming. "Troy, this has got to stop. You don't remember anything anymore. You don't pay any attention to me, don't even sleep with me. Why the hell are we together?"

She was trying to talk this out, but I wasn't having any. I stood in the living room weaving, somewhere in a cloud trying to focus on her standing there in her sheer nightie. "Come on into bed, I'm horny."

That was the worst thing I could have said. The neighbors must have heard her explosion.

She pushed me aside and slammed the bedroom door so hard that the center panel cracked. Suffice it to say, we didn't have sex.

I woke up the next morning lying on the living room floor with the couch cushions pulled on top of me. Cheryl had left for work. I vaguely remembered our argument the previous night and, as usual, dismissed it. We'd had lots of arguments. They blew over like

Seattle's sudden windstorms. I'd come home early tonight, sober, and take her out to dinner. I loved her. She loved me. All couples have spats. The problem would be solved once again.

That evening, I sensed something was very wrong before I opened the apartment door. The living room was empty. No furniture. I rushed into the bedroom. Same thing. Cheryl's clothes were gone. There's nothing more vacuous than a half-empty closet with naked hangers littering the floor.

The stereo and TV were missing. The kitchen was devoid of dishes. Only my few pathetic possessions remained, yearning for companions. She'd emptied the apartment of her belongings during the day. I should have seen it coming. I hadn't. I was too stupid to realize I'd driven her out.

I'd thought my firing by the Chippendales was devastating, but this departure was worse. Far worse! It was an atomic explosion in my mind with a fallout destined to destroy me.

I sank to the carpet, feeling like I was in the middle of the Mojave Desert, sinking into quicksand up to my armpits.

Tears trickled down my cheeks. I'd lost everything now. Why did everyone do these things to me? What had I done to deserve all this shit?

My life was in shambles. I was sitting in the apartment without a fucking thing in it, no Cheryl. Nobody who cared if I lived or died. I didn't either.

The trickles became a flood. I couldn't stop crying. The world was heavy on my shoulders. Unlike Atlas, I hadn't the strength to hold it.

It was the loneliest, worst time of my life. I'd been fired by Chippendales, lost my film career in its infancy, and now had lost Cheryl, the love of my life.

Finally, I looked upward and started praying to God, hoping he would listen, hoping I could hear him tell me what to do, hoping he'd say, "Everything will be all right, Troy."

My cumulus cloud suddenly lifted. God was speaking to me. *Thou must be true to thyself.*

24

After that tormenting day, I wanted to die. I didn't have the nerve to kill myself; I just wanted to pass away in my sleep. The lens through which I saw life fogged before my eyes. When I could finally drop into troubled sleep, I dreamed I was imprisoned on a ship at sea, searching for a distant shore that would forever remain so.

My soul had shipwrecked in an ocean of melancholia. I'd descended to somewhere I didn't want to be, not knowing or caring where that was. I believed I deserved what had happened to me. Ugliness became the horror inside willing me to expel misery onto everyone else.

I focused on myself and how bad I felt. The self-absorption was painful in itself. I felt defeated. All I could think of was how to get rid of the agony, the endless darkness in my mind.

My mood swings were noticed by everyone with whom I came into contact, especially James at work. Thank God for James! He finally convinced me I was the only person who could alter my degraded status. I was forced to re-examine my life. It was an agonizingly brutal self-analysis. Problems so overwhelmed me that I finally admitted that James was right. I needed professional help — immediately.

I found a psychiatrist in Seattle. A couple of sessions later, I was told that I had clinical depression, a dangerous mental disease afflicting millions of people around the world, many of whom (some 18,000 people per year in the United States alone) kill themselves because of it.

That was a frightening enough statistic to force me to follow the psychiatrist's advice and seek out a psychologist for treatment. The psychiatrist recommended a few after prescribing the anti-depressant drug Prozac for me, which I still take daily, four years later.

For my psychologist, I chose Dr. Jane Winslow. She was of Chinese descent, married to a Caucasian man. She was a smallish, studious woman who wore oversized glasses. Her dark hair, cut in a mannish style, matched her persona. She dressed severely in expensive suits or tailored pants outfits in browns or black, nary a splash of color via scarf, belt, or jewelry. Her voice, as strong and soothing as a news commentator's, exuded confidence.

During our first session, Dr. Winslow said that the

fact I had come to her of my own free will was a good sign. Though I was fighting it, thinking counseling wouldn't make any difference in my life, it would. She explained that recognizing the need for help was the first step in recovery.

By the third visit, I felt comfortable enough to tell her about being fired from a glamorous career, omitting most of the details. I'd have to live with a small-town job with no opportunity to do more or better.

She realized the firing was the impetus for accelerating my depression, Cheryl's leaving, the tip of the heaping snow cone to a dangerous state. However, she didn't agree with my assessment of a future.

She explained that I had to learn about myself, about my own identity before I could start to recover. I had to pull myself up from the bottom of the barrel and stop feeling sorry for myself.

She reinforced what the psychiatrist had said, that my emotional state reflected a common problem for many people. I had lost interest in my life. Overwhelming hopelessness and despair had wrapped their tendrils about me like living vines that wouldn't let go. Feelings of worthlessness, self-hate, and excessive guilt added to my misery. It was impossible to find pleasure in any activity or relationship, even those that in the past had provided enjoyment.

During the first months of therapy, I lost my appetite along with fifteen pounds. I was down to my high school weight. Fatigue was a constant companion.

I was failing to cope with my life crisis. My ability to function effectively stopped. Oddly, my depression worked to free me from the life situations that appeared unmanageable.

Although I had thought my depression occurred suddenly, Dr. Winslow explained it had not. The disease had been teasing me for years. My constant insomnia was the clue. Though I'd suspected something mental was going wrong, I hadn't accepted it for what that clue represented.

A year of therapy later, while I was pulling my life together, I saw Ernie on Oprah Winfrey's talk show. He was one of four Chippendale dancers who had been invited to appear on the show. The four did a modified strip which had the audience shouting for more.

The old life. My body tingled with the sicky-sweetness. Thank God, I wasn't a part of it anymore.

Because the show was taped the week previous, I decided to call Ernie. He'd given me his L.A. number before I left Dusseldorf. He might even be there between tours or whatever.

"Hello?"

"Hi, Ernie. It's Troy calling from Seattle."

"Troy? Troy who?"

"You know, Troy Kline, former Chip singer extraordinaire," I joked. "How are you, Ernie?"

"Oh, uh, fine. Listen, Troy, I'm really busy right now. Could you give me a call another time?"

I choked. The brush-off, distinct and deadly as a black widow spider's bite. "Yeah . . . sure. Take care, Ernie." You son of a bitch!

I slammed down the receiver. I never called him back.

The week following that devastating phone call, I asked Dr. Winslow to give me a tentative assessment of my condition and progress. We were in her office at my usual Tuesday session, a deliberately soothing atmosphere of grayness. Soft muted colors adorned the ceiling and drapes. Paintings of landscapes melded with pale walls. No brilliant hues jarred the eye nor drew attention.

She started in slowly. "Depression is an exaggeration of feelings we all experience briefly in our lives, Troy. Someone who is depressed becomes preoccupied with feelings of failure, meaninglessness, and despair. Attempts by others to cheer up the depressed fail because their emptiness is a personal internal experience. It does not match the external reality seen by others. Overwhelming hopelessness has resulted in your cutting off communication with others, in giving up an active effort to take care of yourself or participate in everyday life."

I now understood the symptoms and the cure. I was able to accept my condition and become interested in life again, slowly but surely. I had come a long way from the sobbing hulk sitting in the middle of that empty apartment living room the previous year.

I nodded.

"Troy, your depression is a result of internalized anger and guilt based fundamentally on your upbringing. I'm not speaking just of your religious teachings and its effect on your personal psyche. You rebelled mentally when you were young against the overt display of emotion during religious services. The demonstrative outpouring from participants . . . speaking in tongues, hand-waving, and shouting. All this is spelled out in your present rejection of organized religion.

"Your trip into the wild side of Chippendale life left you ashamed and guilty. You went against all the teachings of your youth. Even your father's statement that if you tithed to the church you wouldn't have financial problems today, had its effect."

I sat in a chair across from her desk, my hands twitching, wanting to light a cigarette even though I'd given up the habit long ago. I wasn't so sure I was ready for this analysis after all.

"You have been unable to manage anger and guilt directly or effectively. You have hidden it, changed it, denied it. You hid it with alcohol, drugs, and promiscuous intercourse, covering up any feelings which could not be dealt with directly with overt actions."

That was exactly what I'd done.

She continued, "Since our thoughts reflect our values and attitudes, these beliefs are also explored in order to understand how current thoughts result in current feelings. In this way, we can learn to change our negative, self-defeating, depressive thoughts, and introduce positive, healthy, and affirmative responses.

"Our thought patterns have a major influence on our feelings. Therefore, we think ourselves into a depression. You have to understand this process and alter your thought patterns. It's called cognitive therapy.

"Your concerns about the circumstances leading to losing your job with Chippendales were the catalyst for your present state.

"You have a big order to fulfill now. Forgive." She paused, allowing the word to sink in. "Forgive your family . . . anyone who has rejected you . . . anyone with whom you still harbor anger. Forgive especially yourself for past deeds, and start a new life, one filled with what I call inner peace."

I felt tears rolling down my cheeks. I couldn't stop them. I didn't want to. I couldn't even lower my eyes from hers.

"Listen to your words, almost a year ago. 'I'll never succeed at anything, because I've failed.' These kinds of thoughts not only facilitate your feelings of depression, they render it difficult for you to work on your self-esteem. They prevent you from seeking a better job or attempting to pursue a singing career . . . which is still a longing in your heart."

She moved around the desk, sat on the corner, and handed me a tissue. "The words are hitting home. That's why you're becoming emotional. There is no shame in emotion. It's what makes us different from our four-legged friends."

After I'd settled down, she returned to her desk chair and started in again. "Several things will help you in your recovery. Continue taking twenty milligrams of Prozac every day. We know the medication has helped. Over the next couple of years, we'll decrease the dosage. As I've said before, continue to eliminate allergenic foods, including sources of caffeine.

"Adopt a regular exercise program. Thirty minutes of physical activity sufficient to elevate the heart rate by fifty percent at least three times a week will do wonders for your libido. It will improve your mood and your ability to handle stress, even help you to get up in the morning and face each day.

"For goodness sake, do not pick up smoking again. You don't need other stimulants to hide your feelings. You must learn to live with those feelings.

"It wouldn't hurt for you to start taking vitamin supplements. Here's a list I recommend." She handed me a typewritten sheet.

She ended the session by telling me how much I'd improved since I started therapy. I was well on the way to recovery, but I shouldn't be surprised if something triggered the depression again in the future.

That was a sobering thought.

After that year of therapy, I could look back and see how much I'd accomplished. Such reflection motivated me more and more. My new attitude was the catalyst for building a good clientele base at Hair Company. I was dating some.

Following Dr. Winslow's advice, I became involved in group therapy once a week for another year.

I learned not to talk about my depression and resultant therapy to anyone other than the therapy group. People look upon someone seeing a psychologist as someone diseased. In the public eye, shame is still attached to mental illness. Does anyone want to get involved with the diseased? I don't think so.

I moved on with my life, taking those small steps.

25

Today, at 32, I am functioning with inner peace, a reflection of how I feel about myself. It's the glue that keeps me bound and ticking. I don't have to rely on illegal drugs or alcohol to keep the home fires burning.

I've dated only two girls in the past year, having turned a new page in my life, one without the need for casual sex.

One-night stands are better left to others. I've had more than my share, believe me.

I spend a lot of time with Rene, nine years old now. We're closer than ever. I'm a good father, spending every other weekend with her. In the summer, she spends several weeks here in Issaquah with me. I take her to the park, and shopping, and Village Theater productions. We participate in activities she enjoys.

I also do volunteer work, cutting hair every week

or so for Friends of Youth, a Seattle-area group that assists abused children. It's a cause that's important to me, and I'm able to give back some of the things God granted me.

I intend to fill my new book with pages of someone with whom to spend the rest of my life. I'd like more children, a house with a white picket fence, all the accouterments in which I had little or no interest previously.

Today, after analyzing my stint with Chippendales, I feel the firing by Mark Pakin was a blessing from God. It removed me from a lifestyle bent on my self-destruction. The glamorous calling was my downfall, even though it was filled with frantic possibilities of which I hadn't the judgment to take advantage. If I could have handled the notoriety of being a Chippendale without involving myself in all the pot and promiscuity, perhaps I could have furthered my singing career.

My religious upbringing, obviously in the forefront of my mind throughout the tour, wracked my body with guilt which I could not ignore. Lack of that acknowledgment came home to roost in the form of several years of clinical depression and a need for therapy that couldn't be denied.

Everyone thinks that with fame and money comes happiness. Tabloids are choked with articles about celebrities who achieve stardom, then fall from grace even faster due to excesses. Though I didn't reach stardom or fame nor achieve riches, it was a test run that I hope others avoid. I would suggest any young person embarking on such an adventure be aware of the possible consequences, tread lightly, and understand fully what evils lie in that pit.

I do cherish the opportunity of finding my worth as a professional singer. Large audiences appreciated my voice and style. I know now that I am good. My voice is still strong, my musical ability intact. However, singing isn't the priority it used to be in my life. I sing in church and for friends.

In the past few years, I failed to devote myself to anything a hundred percent. It wasn't until a year and a half ago that I finally pulled my act together. Now, I'm at peace. In truth, I've forgiven myself and everyone else and am living for the future, ready to embrace life as it is dealt.

Though reality was difficult to embrace after being on such a five-month high, I've worked hard to improve, a fact that shows through to new people I meet today. I am tolerant and understanding of those of all races, religious beliefs, or sexual preference, even those with drug or alcohol addictions.

Now that I've accomplished a certain amount of personal growth, I am striving for spiritual growth as well. My relationship with God is renewed. I've developed my own special relationship with Him. It's as though during my earlier life I was on a roller coaster, using God as a rail car to help me through the climbs and runaway plunges and ignoring him during the straightaways. I no longer walk blindly through life ignoring consequences of wrongdoings.

If I ever become successful as a singer, I'll know how to prevent myself from diving into the pool of self-destruction.

I have the confidence to approach life's avarice with a humbleness that I couldn't have even imagined previously. I'll handle any success with humility and caring for other people around me.

After all, "who am I to judge someone for the splinter they have in their eye when I have a plank in mine?"

THE END

Gillespie, Marcia Ann. "A Different Take on the Ol' Bump and Grind," *Ms.*, October 1987.

Grubb, Kevin. "Broadway and Beyond," Dance, September 1987.

Weinberg, Janie S., and Richard A. Friend. "Depression," *Au Courant.*

"Chippendales: A New Experience," *That's Entertainment International's ShowBiz,* August 1987.

"Depression," *Diagnostic and Statistical Manual of Mental Disorders (DSM-III),* American Psychiatric Association.